DEATH   AND   EUTHANASIA

IN

JEWISH   LAW

STUDIES IN PROGRESSIVE HALAKHAH, VOLUME IV

Also in this Series

Walter Jacob and Moshe Zemer (eds.) DYNAMIC JEWISH LAW,
Progressive Halakhah - Essence and Application

Walter Jacob and Moshe Zemer (eds.) RABBINIC - LAY
RELATIONS IN JEWISH LAW

Walter Jacob and Moshe Zemer (eds.) CONVERSION TO JUDAISM
IN JEWISH LAW - Essays and Responsa

AFFILIATED WITH THE WORLD UNION
FOR
PROGRESSIVE JUDAISM

DEATH AND EUTHANASIA

IN JEWISH LAW

Essays and Responsa

Edited by
Walter Jacob and Moshe Zemer

Freehof Institute of Progressive Halakhah
Pittsburgh and Tel Aviv
Rodef Shalom Press
1995

Published by the Rodef Shalom Press
4905 Fifth Avenue
Pittsburgh, PA 15213
U.S.A.

4905 5th Avenue
Pittsburgh, PA 15213
U.S.A.

4 Rehov Levitan
69204 Tel Aviv
Israel

Library of Congress Catalog Card Number 94-68867

Jacob, Walter 1930-

Zemer, Moshe 1932-

ISBN 0-929699-06-8

This volume is dedicated
to
the memory of

Stanley H. Levin   ז״ל

and

Dr. Jacob Mittelmann   ז״ל

CONTENTS

PREFACE

We continue to be grateful to the Rodef Shalom Congregation for supporting the Freehof Institute of Progressive *Halakhah* and its assistance in technical matters connected with the publication of this volume. We wish to thank Barbara Bailey for her efforts with the typescript as well as Douglas Szalla and Svetlana Geguzina for their help. Our thanks to Rabbi Daniel Schiff and Irene Jacob who assisted with the proof reading.

INTRODUCTION

Problems associated with death and dying have always been with us, but they have assumed a somewhat different form in recent years. There are a number of reasons for this. The enormous advances of medical science in the last century has led to increased expectations. The patient and the family feel that surely something else can be done, and that medical technology which is changing so rapidly must be able to provide answers which will save the individual threatened by death. These expectations have often proved to be correct as new and untried medical techniques have been used to help thousands of patients around the world and particularly in our highly advanced medical community.

There are, of course, limits beyond which even the best medical technology cannot go, and when those are reached disappointment was bound to be felt. That along with an arrogance on the part of some medical practitioners who believed that all decisions were now in their hands has led to a reexamination of medical ethics particularly at critical junctures when death threatened. Rather than permitting the physician to make decisions alone, the patients and their families have wanted to be included in the process. They have, of course, sought advice from many sources including the religious community as they wished to do what was good for the patient and what was right and ethical.

An additional set of problems has been raised by the continued use of medical technology when it no longer could benefit the patient. In some instances this has been done at the request of the patients or their families. In others, it has simply occurred because it was available and has become standard procedure irrespective of the condition or potential for life in the patient. Added to all of this has been the fear of litigations by the medical profession, something which has become a major factor in the last years.

These issues and others have raised questions which Judaism must answer. The traditional responsa have been only partially helpful because few individuals have reviewed them in the light of the new medical technology and/or changed attitudes. Furthermore, the number of discussions about these matter in the past remains extremely limited.

There are only a handful of examples from the Talmudic period and most serious discussions occurred only in the nineteenth century during a time when traditional Judaism felt embattled, and so tended to make negative responses to all questions which sought any change in attitude.

The nucleus of this volume consists of papers delivered at an international symposium of the Institute of Progressive *Halakhah* in Montreal in 1993. Several papers have been enlarged and some have been added.

Although a number of Reform responsa on this subject have appeared over the decades, there has been no thorough examination of the question of death and euthanasia since a lengthy essay/responsum by Jacob Z. Lauterbach, in 1924. The essays in this volume seek to examine the problem of death and euthanasia in the light of both tradition and our modern understanding of the *halakhah*. The responsa provided in this volume are representative of what has been written during this century.

WITHDRAWING OR WITHHOLDING NUTRITION, HYDRATION OR OXYGEN FROM PATIENTS

Mark N. Staitman

Jews are unusually large consumers of medical care. We are quick to call upon the expertise of the physician to cure. Because of medical advances we live longer, and much which might have killed us in an earlier time is now curable. Among the most difficult issues facing the liberal Jew is the issue of medical care at the "end stages of life." The "end stages of life" are no longer well defined. Generally we are familiar with the non-Jewish thought on this issue, but have little knowledge of Jewish thought. Positions held by liberal Jews tend to be reflective of the non-Jewish thinking. This is not difficult to understand. The "popular literature" has had little discussion of the "end stages of life" from a Jewish perspective. Even the most popular periodicals in the Jewish community have carried have hardly concerned themselves with the issue.

This paper will first discuss the reasons why the non-Jewish categories and paradigms for approaching this issue are inadequate for liberal Jews. The paper will define a theology which allows for a liberal Jewish approach to the issue and then apply this theology to the issue of the treatment of Jewish patients in a persistent vegetative state.

Most non-Jewish discussion of the issue of treatment during the "end stages of life" comes from Catholic moral theology. Catholicism argues that God alone is absolute. Life was created and redeemed by God, but life itself is not absolute. Physical life serves as a condition of the fulfillment of other purposes, (the love of God, love of neighbor, etc.). Life should be protected and preserved. Its sovereignty is delegated to humanity, but it is limited and conditional. Some killing is permissible, and indeed, in some instanced, required. When then is this sovereignty delegated to humanity?

Christian ethics determined a set of norms which defined when a human being could morally cause an end to life. This led to thinking about killing in moral categories. A concrete example of norms of killing would be the "Just War Theory" which enunciates the principle that it is always wrong to take an innocent human life directly. This led to the categories of "direct" and "innocent." In the area of bioethics, Christianity has developed the norm of "ordinary vs. extraordinary."

> ...normally one is held to use only ordinary means-according to circumstances of persons, places, times, and culture-that is to say, means that do not involve any grave burden for oneself or another. A more strict obligation would be too burdensome for most men and would render the attainment of the higher, more important good too difficult. Life, health, all temporal activities are in fact subordinated to spiritual ends.[1]

Clearly, from the statement of Pope Pius XII, "ordinary means" are determined by time, place and culture. "Extraordinary means" would be those which are too burdensome or those "which would render the attainment of the higher, more important good too difficult." "Ordinary means" must be both useful (efficacious) and convenient. Much which might have been "extraordinary" a few years ago might today be "ordinary." Much of what might have been burdensome or inconvenient a few years ago might now be convenient.

Another applicable norm of Christianity is "autonomy." The Christian discussion of the taking of life begins with the issue of one's "right" to act in such a way. By what right can a person act to deprive another of life? After all, if life is conditional and not absolute, then there must be instances when an individual can morally act to deprive another of life. If a person has no autonomy and is "owned" by God, than the decision to deprive one of life can only be that of God. If one is autonomous, then he or she takes full responsibility for moral choice, and one then has complete control over one's body.[2]

These categories and paradigms are inadequate for a liberal Jewish discussion of the issues. Judaism does not understand life as relative. Judaism understands all human life to be of infinite value, i.e.

absolute.[3] Life was created by God, but given to humanity. Physical life serves as the earthly medium for the relationship between God and the individual. This relationship manifests itself in the covenant between God and humanity. For the Jewish people, this covenant is expressed through the performance of *mitzvot*. It is not that life serves as a condition of the fulfillment of other purposes, but rather, that life finds its meaning in the expression of the covenant with God. Life is meaningful when it is in relationship. For that relationship to be one of freedom, the sovereignty must be humanity's. God must "give up control" (*kivyakhol*). Ultimately then, determination of when human beings can cause an end to life must be determined by human beings, but within the context of the covenant. Capital punishment, killing in war, killing in self defense and the like, are all examples of taking life in the context of the covenant. Those whose behavior is such that it threatens the continuation of the covenantal relationship with God, or whose behavior is such that it precludes others from performing *mitzvot* are at risk of losing their lives because of the freedom and sovereignty of humanity. The categories of "direct" "innocent" "ordinary" and "extraordinary" have no theological basis in Judaism. So too "quality of life," a category rooted in relativist theology.

Traditional Judaism believes that God "owns" the individual. One's life is the possession of God, and thus, even though humanity has the freedom to act in the world. that freedom is limited by the conditions of the covenant, i.e. the *mitzvot*. While God has given humanity freedom, it is a freedom limited by the structure of the *mitzvot*. Liberal Judaism has rejected the idea that God "owns" the individual. It sees the autonomy of the individual freely limited by the individual in order to be in relationship. The individual Jew must then take full responsibility for moral choice, and one then has complete control over her or his body.[4]

Both Traditional Judaism and Liberal Judaism have struggled with the issues of defining death and euthanasia. Both have tried to adapt to modern scientific standards and criteria for determining death. Liberal *halakhists* have accepted various criteria for defining "brain

3

death." Some Orthodox *posqim* have accepted "brain stem death" as an appropriate criterion for defining death. Others have adhered to the traditional definition of death as cessation of respiration and heart beat.[5] Both Liberal and Orthodox *posqim* have rejected the use of active euthanasia.[6]

Neither Liberal nor Orthodox *posqim* have written on the treatment of those in a persistent vegetative state. The *Tzitz Eliezer* does discuss the issue of withholding or withdrawing nutrition or hydration from patients who are terminally ill. He argues that even with respect to a *goses* one cannot withhold nutrition or hydration. How much the more so with one who is terminal, but not expected to die within three days. The published responsa of the CCAR, Rabbi Walter Jacob or Rabbi Solomon B. Freehof do not deal with those in a persistent vegetative state. As the condition of the persistent vegetative state is among the hardest for families, and presents new and difficult issues for Liberal Judaism as it attempts to understand the end stages of life, we ought to address this issue. What must one provide for those in a persistent vegetative state? What is the theological basis for this understanding?

A persistent vegetative state is, for this paper, defined as a state in which the individual has only brain stem function. Brain stem function controls only the autonomic reflexes, but not cognition nor the five senses. Those in a persistent vegetative state have no possibility of ever again regaining cognition or the five senses. Those in a persistent vegetative state cannot eat, drink, respond to pain, sound or other stimuli, or have the possibility of ever responding to these stimuli. Those in a persistent vegetative state receive nutrition and hydration through intravenous or indwelling "feeding" tubes. An individual in a persistent vegetative state is not a *goses*. A *goses* is one who is expected to die within 72 hours. This person in a persistent vegetative state could continue to breath for months or years.

Traditional Judaism would prohibit the withholding or

4

withdrawing of nutrition or hydration from patients in a persistent vegetative state. If such a patient were in need of a respirator, or had been placed on a respirator, traditional Judaism would permit withholding the use of the respirator (and Moshe Tendler has devised a way for withdrawing the use of an already placed respirator). The reason for the difference between the permissibility of withholding artificial means of respiration and artificial means of nutrition and hydration has to do with the theological understanding of breathing as opposed to eating and drinking. Breathing is understood as a basic criterion of life. It is God's "breathing the breath of life" into *Adam HaRishon* which gives life to all humanity. The inability to sustain respiration independently indicates the inability to live. The respirator does not sustain life, but delays death. It has much the same status as the chopping sound which prevents the *goses* from dying. Removing the sound allows the individual to slip into that peaceful blissful sleep.[7]

While the natural course of events is that one ceases to breath and thus is dead, this is not the case with nutrition and hydration. The inability to eat or drink is not a criterion for determining death. Depriving one of the artificial induction of nutrition and hydration is understood as taking positive steps to kill an individual, not allowing death to occur.

Finally, specifically addressing the issue of intravenous feedings for terminally ill patients, Rabbi Feinstein says that "for an incurably ill patient who had difficulty breathing, I have already stated that one must give him oxygen to relieve his suffering. It is also clear that such a patient who cannot eat normally must be fed intravenously, since such feeding strengthens the patient somewhat even if the patient does not feel anything, (i.e., is comatose). Food is not at all comparable to medication, since food is a natural substance which all living creatures require to maintain life."[8]

Secular medical ethics does not draw a distinction among respiration, nutrition and hydration. All three are necessary for life.

5

Without any one of the three, life cannot be sustained. If then there is a moral reason for providing any one of these three, there is a moral basis for providing all three.

Liberal Judaism is uncomfortable with the theology which draws a distinction between respiration and nutrition or hydration, but is equally uncomfortable with the secular medical ethical position. This is clearly seen in the case of the frail elderly. Mrs. Ginsberg, a ninety-two year old nursing home patient is visited daily by her son and daughter. She talks weekly with her grandchildren by telephone. Most liberal Jews would be comfortable with a "Do Not Resuscitate" order for Mrs. Ginsburg. Mrs. Ginsburg does not want to be placed on a respirator. She does not wish to live with the limitations of no longer being able to communicate with her family. She is afraid that if she is placed on a respirator, she will lose all control over her care, and will lose the ability to communicate. On a respirator she will be in a "state of indignity." If she goes into respiratory failure, she wishes to be allowed to die. Death would be within a few hours. As Mrs. Ginsburg gets older, it is more and more difficult for her to eat and drink. She can no longer chew, and swallowing has become difficult. None the less, she is lucid and communicative. She might well be sustained on a feeding tube. Without a feeding tube, she would die within a few weeks. Some how nutrition and hydration seem different from respiration. Both the length of time between the withdrawal or withholding of therapy and death, and the nature of the death seem to make Jews uncomfortable. While Mrs. Ginsburg is not in a persistent vegetative state, her case does help us to see the difference in the way we experience and react to mechanical ventilation as opposed to mechanically administered nutrition and hydration.

Prior to the twentieth century there were no patients in persistent vegetative states. The various cerebral accidents which lead to this state were untreatable in earlier times. Before to the development of intravenous hydration and nutrition, patients died. Prior to the development of the ventilator patients died. Because there is no

6

precedent for the treatment of those in a persistent vegetative state, the *halakhah* had to look to other cases from which a parallel could be drawn. Some suggest we find a parallel in the *goses*. This is most unfortunate because the *goses* is clearly not a parallel. The *goses* is expected to die within three days. The *goses* is considered a living being for all purposes. "What is the difference between ill people and *gosesin*? The majority of ill patients live, while the majority of *gosesin* die."[9] While all patients in a persistent vegetative state will eventually die, they will not of necessity die from this condition unless it goes untreated. Some have attempted to draw a parallel between the *terefah* and the patient in a persistent vegetative state. This too is unfortunate because the *terefah* is a terminally ill patient who will die of his disease. Maimonides, in his *Mishneh Torah*, states "One who murders a *terefah*, even though he eats and drinks and walks about the market, he is exempt from human judgment. All human beings are under the presumption of being healthy and one who murders is put to death unless it is known with certainty that the one murdered was a *terefah* and doctors testify that this illness had no cure and the person would have died from this, if not from something else first."[10] The patient in a persistent vegetative state is not a *terefah* for a persistent vegetative state is not a terminal illness. Where then is a parallel to be found?

One possibility for a parallel might be found in the *Talmud*. "R. Judah said in the name of Shmuel, if the neck bone and the major portion of the surrounding flesh was broken, the body immediately defiles in the tent."[11] Maimonides, in his *Mishneh Torah* states, "A dead person does not cause ritual impurity until the soul has departed. Even if one is bleeding to death or a *goses*...If he broke his neck bone and the greater part of the surrounding flesh or if his back were ripped like that of a fish, or if he were decapitated or his belly broken into two parts he is rendered ritually unclean, even if he still trembles in one of his limbs."[12] The *halakhah* joined the individual who was decapitated with the one whose neck bone was broken. Why? What do these individuals have in common? The person who was decapitated is, for all *posqim*, dead. There was no possibility of recovery. While limbs might twitch

7

or shake, the rabbis understood this to be a simple muscular reaction, not an indication of any life. While Maimonides did not discuss the moment of the soul's departure and how to determine it, he clearly understood that this twitching headless body was soulless, and thus lifeless. But not so the individual with the broken neck. While it is unlikely that this person would live long, the moment following the accident would not of necessity be the moment of the "departing of the soul." We can imagine the modern case of an automobile accident where one passenger is decapitated, while another has his or her neck shattered and the flesh ripped open. Upon reaching the scene of the accident paramedics would likely begin a triage process. The decapitated individual would be ignored, for there is nothing to be done. The person with the broken neck might well be looking at the paramedic. Eyes stare, though no sound can be made. All voluntary movement is prevented by the spinal cord injury. None the less, the paramedics begin to work. An IV is started, blood pressure is taken, and transportation arranged to the trauma unit. At the trauma unit the patient is placed on a ventilator, a cardiac assist and an EEG is taken. After a few hours brain stem activity ceases, and the family is consulted about the deceased being an organ donor. At the moment of the accident this individual was not dead. The status of this individual was qualitatively different from the status of the decapitated person. The decapitated person was dead. The person with the broken neck was dying. How do we understand this "dying"? What is the common quality of both of these individuals which allows the *halakhah* to see them as the same?

Maimonides uses the term *sheteitzei nafsho* as the designation of death. The departure of the soul becomes the moment of death, and the definition of a corpse a "soulless body." This "soulless body" differs from the animated body in that it no longer can be in relationship with God. The soulless body can no longer perform *mitzvot*. The theological significance of death is that the covenant between God and this previously animated person now must be enacted in some other plane (perhaps the *olam habah)*. There are many categories of individuals who cannot perform *mitzvot* and who live in a state of an unfulfilled covenant.

8

Infants, who cannot yet perform *mitzvot*, the profoundly retarded, anencephalic newborns, comatose patients, and patients in a persistent vegetative state are all in a state where it is impossible to perform *mitzvot* and thus, to participate in the covenant. There is, however, a difference among categories. Some have the potential of performing *mitzvot*. Others of these categories have no possibility of ever being able to perform *mitzvot*. The new born will grow and learn. Prayer, study, *tzedaqah* and travel to Israel may all become a part of life. The profoundly retarded may at some time have some self consciousness and express, even silently, a prayer. The comatose patient may hear the *shema* and internally respond. Not so the patient in a persistent vegetative state. This patient lacks all brain function other than brain stem function. There can be no cognition nor any experience of the five senses. Not only can this patient not perform *mitzvot*, there is no potential for ever performing *mitzvot*. In a sense we can say that this patient no longer has a soul. Like the decapitated or the one with the broken neck bone, this one cannot, and never will again perform *mitzvot*. The very basis for the relationship with God through the covenant, the very source of meaning in life is now gone.

This new category of existence, a breathing body which has no potential for the performance of *mitzvot*, is disturbing . How ought we behave toward such a patient? We have clear obligations toward this patient, as we do to all human beings, dead or alive. Recognizing the basic dignity (*kavod*) of the individual, we must treat this new category of person with honor and care. We cannot mutilate it nor can we derive benefit from it, (with the possible exception of *piquah nefesh*). While clearly this category is different from a corpse, it is also different from a *goses* or a *terefah*. While there may be an obligation to provide hydration and nutrition to a *goses*, there is no obligation to provide ventilation to such a patient. Ventilation would not prolong life, but rather, prevent the dying process from proceeding. The need for artificial ventilation defines a point at which the dying process has reached an irreversible point for the *goses*. For the patient in a persistent vegetative state theological death has already occurred. The

9

permanent, irreversible inability to perform *mitzvot* gives this person the same theological status as the decapitated person or the one with the broken neck bone. Just as there is no obligation to provide any form of medical treatment to either of these individuals, so there is no obligation to provide treatment to the patient in the persistent vegetative state. Nutrition, hydration and artificial ventilation may be withheld or withdrawn.

Notes

1. Pope Pius XII "The Prolongation of Life", An Address to an International Congress of Anesthesiologists, 24 November 1957, *The Pope Speaks* 4 (1957) pp. 395-396. Quoted in Lisa Sowle Cahill, "Respecting Life and Causing Death in the Medical Context", in J. Pohier and D. Mieth, eds., *Suicide and the Right to Die*, Edinburgh, 1985.

2. For a full discussion see "Perspectives from Catholic Theology" by Reverend Edward J. Bayer, S.T.D. in Joanne Lynn, MD., *By No Extraordinary Means*, Bloomington, 1986, pp. 89-98.

3. See especially Fred Rosner, *Modern Medicine and Jewish Ethics*, New York, 1991, pp. 274ff.

4. Much of this theology comes from Eugene B. Borowitz. His *Renewing the Covenant*, Philadelphia, 1991, has been particularly influential in my thinking.

5. See Rosner, pp. 263-277.

6. The liberal Jewish sources discuss these issues in various responsa. The key sources are *Reform Responsa For Our Time #17, American Reform Responsa #76, 77, 78* and *79* (note also the discussion following #78), *Questions and Reform Jewish Answers #156, 159,* and *160*. Traditional Jewish sources include *Tzitz Eliezer* 14, 80. The *Tzitz Eliezer* summarizes the positions of others, and presents his own position.

7. *Shulhan Arukh, Yoreh Deah* 339:1.

8. Moshe Feinstein quoted in Rosner, p. 240.

9. *b. Qiddushin* 71b.

10. *Mishneh Torah, Hilkhot Rotzeah* 2:8

11. *b. Hullin* 21a.

12. *Mishneh Torah, Hilkhot Tumat HaMet* 1:15

10

EUTHANASIA

Leonard Kravitz

Euthanasia is, as everybody knows, a word that is taken from the Greek, from *eu* 'easy' and *thanatos* 'death'.[1] As everybody, perhaps, may not know, there is a parallel Hebrew term found in the *Talmud*; it is *mitah yafah*, "a nice death".[2] We find the term in the discussion of a judicial execution; the Talmud tells us that we should choose for the condemned criminal "a nice death" and thus fulfill the commandment, "Thou shalt love thy neighbor as thyself" (Lev.19:25). What is a 'nice death'? Rashi tells us: *sheyamut maher*, "that he should die quickly". A nice death is to die quickly; to die slowly, we may deduce, is to die an ugly death. For the condemned, to die quickly is to suffer less; to die slowly is to suffer more.

The connection between time and suffering brings us to the issue of euthanasia. Were the dying person not suffering, were that person perfectly comfortable, in possession of his/her faculties, the issue would never arise! Suffering causes it to arise. Every human being, after all, every day and every moment, moves toward the grave; if life be free from suffering and full of delight, who would think of speeding there? Euthanasia presents itself as an option only when a person is dying *and* suffering and there seems no possibility of reversing the first condition or palliating the second. The two elements of euthanasia, then, are death, death which is imminent, and suffering, suffering which can't be controlled.

Much has been written on the Jewish attitude toward euthanasia. Handbooks of Jewish medical ethics are filled with statements proclaiming that Judaism opposes euthanasia:

> One may not hasten death, even that of a patient who is suffering greatly and for whom there is no hope of a cure, even if the patient asks that this be done. To shorten the life of a person, even a life of agony and suffering, is forbidden...[I]t is equivalent to murder and is punishable accordingly.[3]

and   It is clear, then, that, even when the patient is already known to be on his deathbed and close to the end, any form of *active euthanasia* is strictly prohibited. In fact, it is condemned as plain murder.[4]

and   In all its stringency, this question confronts us with that which touches on the very essence of the mission of the physician, whose sole assignment is to heal as stated in the Torah *rapo y'rapeh* (Ex.21:19) to heal and in no way and in no manner to kill...[5]

and   The practice of euthanasia - whether active or passive - is contrary to the teachings of Judaism. Any positive act designed to hasten the death of the patient is equated with murder in Jewish law...No matter how laudable the intentions of the person performing the act of mercy-killing may be, his deed constitutes an act of homicide...Only the Creator, who bestows the gift of life, may relieve man of that life, even when it has become a burden rather than a blessing.[6]

With such certain statements about euthanasia, one might have expected that there would be a plethora of textual bases for such a view. In truth, there are but two *Talmudic* texts which are adduced and it is their interpretation which has been the basis of the aforementioned Jewish view of euthanasia. There is a *Midrashic* passage which raises substantial questions about that view. There is also a passage in a post-*Talmudic* tractate and a reflection on that passage in a commentary on the *Shulhan Arukh*.

12

We propose to reexamine these texts. We shall suggest that they do not support the notions that have been loaded upon them. Sloganeering has made reflection on these texts and those values said to emerge from them more difficult. At times we may wonder whether it is the urge to make an edifying statement or mere cognative dissonance that has allowed people to say that Judaism views human life as a primary value, [7] all the while knowing that the *Mishnah* describes four methods of execution and that Judaism is not a pacifist tradition.

The first three texts which we will consider relate to events in the lives of *Tannaim* who lived in the second and third century C.E.[8] Taking the two *Talmudic* texts first in the presumptive order of the lives of the *Tannaim* mentioned, we have an account of the execution of Hananiah ben Teryadion and the story of the last days of Judah the Prince, called Rabbi. The *Midrashic* passage will tell of an event in the life of Rabbi Yose. What we shall discover is that as important as the rabbis are in the stories, more important are other figures who appear. Hence we may characterize these texts and the events depicted as "the kind executioner", "the troubled maid", and "the surprising old lady".

The first text is often quoted as providing the basis of the Jewish view of euthanasia. It deals with the cruel execution by burning of Hananiah ben Teradyion. Arrested for teaching Torah, he was to be made an example by the Romans. Hence they determined that he should suffer horribly before he died. So they bound scrolls of the Law to him, piled boughs around him, and ignited them all. But lest the fire kill him too quickly, the Romans placed wet mats of wool about his body. Rabbi Hananiah's students said to him

> Rabbi...open your mouth that the fire may enter [and you die]. He said to them, 'It is better that He who gave my soul should take it and let no one harm himself. The executioner asked him, 'Rabbi if I intensify the fire and remove the mats from your body will you bring me in to

the World to Come?' He said, 'Yes'. 'Swear to me'[said the executioner]. He swore to him. He [the executioner] immediately removed the mats and increased the flames. His [Hananiah's] soul speedily departed. Then he [the executioner] leaped up and fell into the fire. A *bat kol* went out and proclaimed:"Rabbi Hananiah and the executioner are prepared for the Life to Come. Rabbi [Jehudah Ha-Nasi] wept and said, 'Some may attain their world in [but] one moment while others may take many years.[9]

Rabbi Hananiah's response to his students has been taken as the exemplar of the Jewish attitude toward euthanasia.[10] "It is better than He who gave my soul should take it" has been taken as indicating that only God should end life and that no one else may intrude in the dying process.Indeed, "let no one harm himself" is taken as an injunction against anything that would speed that process.[11]

However, when one looks at the story again, one notes that it does not present one consistent position. Since the story purports to present events occuring *over time*, it may well be that enduring the suffering that he did, Rabbi Hananiah *changed his mind* and facilitated his own death! Surely the speech of the kind executioner as given is not to be taken as a mere request for information, nor was Rabbi Hananiah's response the giving of that information; it was a *contract*! The fact that the executioner asked Rabbi Hananiah to swear to it, indicates that both the executioner and the rabbi knew what was to be the outcome and what was to be the *quid pro quo*.[12]

The question then is did Rabbi Hananiah "hasten his death"?[13] It would seem that he did! He could have remained silent or he could have said to the executioner, if you are asking for information, that is one thing, but if you are asking for my concurrence, that is another thing, for I will remain consistent with my earlier statement and I will

14

do nothing which might even seem to speed my death. Of course, Hananiah did not remain silent nor did he say what I have suggested he could have said. It would have been, it is true, inhuman to expect him to have followed either alternative. It is human and expected to have him do what he did do: faced by certain death and experiencing terrible pain, Hananiah sought to avoid the latter by accelerating the former.

Looking at the story of the death of Rabbi Judah the Prince, we shall find, to say the least, an acceleration of the dying process. We read that when Rabbi was very ill, approaching death, the Sages proclaimed a fast, made an appeal for Divine mercy, and announced that anyone who said that Rabbi was dying would be thrust through with a sword. The story continues with the actions of Rabbi's maid:

> The maid of Rabbi went up to the roof. She said, 'Those on high are seeking Rabbi and those below are seeking Rabbi. [Those below, Rabbi's students are praying that he live, even as the powers on high are moving that he die]. May it be God'swill that those below conquer those on high!' [However] when she saw how many times he [Rabbi] would take off and put on his *tefillin* as he would enter the privy and how he was suffering, she said, 'Would that those on high would win against those below'. However, the rabbis did not cease imploring God's mercy. She, then, took a vase and threw it from the roof. They [the Rabbis] were interrupted in their prayer [lit. they were silenced in their requesting God's mercy] and Rabbi's soul departed.[14]

The actions of the troubled maid relate to the assumptions of the story: prayer was believed to be a mechanism of maintaining the life of Rabbi; it was also believed that prayer might be used to ask for his death. What is striking in the story of the maid is that she did more than pray; she *acted* and she acted *physically*: she threw the pot down from the roof. She interrupted the prayer of his students which kept Rabbi alive; she interfered with Rabbi's life support system. She acted; he died. One may say that she enabled him to die or one may say that she caused him to die; in either case, her act precipitated his death.[15]

One should also note that the actions of the maid were operative *without reference* to the wishes of the old man himself. The story tells us that *she* concludes by looking at his actions that he is in pain. We did not hear from the story his own evaluation of his pain. The story suggests, then that one may be able to determine another's level of pain by observing his actions. The story also suggests that one may act upon that observation, since in no way do we find the actions of the maid condemned. Even though death was speeded for the suffering old man we do not read in the *Talmud* text following that story that which we will read in another text, namely, that "...Jewish Law...cannot... purchase relief from pain and misery at the cost of life itself."[16]

As noted, the death of Rabbi did not follow, at least from the story, from his own request. There is a rabbinic text which tells of a person requesting and receiving advice on ending one's life. It should be further noted that this is not a story of death ending great pain; perhaps it is better described as death ending ennui; prayer as a life maintaining mechanism figures in it:

> There is a story of a woman who grew very old. She came before R. Yose (Ha-galili) ben Halafta. She said to him, 'Rabbi, I have gotten too old. Life is repugnant to me; I can taste neither food nor drink. I would like to depart from this world.' He said to her, 'How is it that you have lived so long?' She answered, 'Every day, I am accustomed to go early to the synagogue, even if I must leave something I like'. He said to her, 'Refrain for three successive days from going to the synagogue.' She went and did this. On the third day, she became ill and died.[17]

16

It should be noted, again, that the Sage to whom this suprising old lady went did not upbraid her nor did he proclaim to her Judaism's opposition to euthanasia. He simply asked her why she lived so long.On the basis of her reply, he devised a plan by which she might bring that life to an end.

In both stories, that of Rabbi and that of the old lady, prayer is held to be a life-maintaining mechanism and the interruption or cessation of prayer becomes the means of ending life. Time plays a role in both stories, time and suffering in the first instance and time and an unchanged condition in the second. In the story of Rabbi, the maid is praying that the suffering man live; then time passes and she is praying that the suffering man die;then time passes and that prayer is seen not to be efficacious and the maid acts by dropping the vase. In the story of the old lady, she has three days to consider the advice of Rabbi Jose and to reconsider her desire to terminate her life. From the story, one may assume that had she changed her mind before the three *successive* days were up, she would have lived!

Both stories [and the second part of the story of Rabbi Hananiah] suggest in a negative fashion that the notion that Judaism has always and everywhere been opposed to euthanasia simply cannot be maintained. Indeed, the disparity between what has been claimed as Judaism's position and what these three texts say leads one to wonder what has been the basis for that position. If anything, the three stories, in different ways, remind us of Rashi's definition of *mitah yafah sheyamut maher*, that one dies quickly, quicker than one might die otherwise!

Semahot is a post *Talmudic* tractate which presents the case of the *goses,* the person who is at the point of death but who is still alive.[18] It would seem that the *halakhic* treatment of the *goses* provides more of a base for the so-called Jewish view of euthanasia than the three aforementioned texts.About the *goses* we learn that he

17

... is regarded as a living entity in respect to all matters of the world... We do not tie up his cheek-bones, or stop up his apertures, or place a metal vessel or anything which chills on his navel, as it is stated, 'Before the silver cord is snapped asunder and the golden bowl is shattered, and the pitcher is broken at the fountain' (Ecc. 12:6)... We may not move him, or place him on sand or salt until he dies... We may not close the eyes of a dying man. Whoever touches and moves him is a murderer. For R. Meir used to say: He can be compared to a lamp which is dripping, should a man touch it he extinguishes it. Similarly whoever closes the eyes of a dying man is considered to have taken his life.[19]

Though according to the *Semahot* one may do nothing to speed the departure of the soul of the *goses*, according to a later authority the *Ramah*, one may do something to remove any impediment to that departure, thus

...if there is anything which causes a hindrance to the departure of the soul, such as the presence near the patient's house of a knocking noise, such as wood chopping, or if there is salt on the patient's tongue, and these hinder the soul's departure, it is permissible to remove them from there because there is no act involved with this at all but only the removal of the impediment.[20]

These two passages raise questions about what has been called active and passive euthanasia.[21] While the first passage prohibits any action which would bring death quicker, the second mandates actions which do. Yet in truth, one cannot truly call the "removal of the impediment" a *passive* action; one must go to the wood chopper to tell him to stop and one must reach into the patient's mouth to remove the salt. There is certainly an "act involved"! It should be clear that we do

18

not enter into the question whether in fact rhythmic sounds or salt on the tongue prolong life; we simply point to the fact that stopping the former or removing the latter are *actions done* and not actions refrained from being done. If at this moment, the sounds and the salt are keeping the patient alive, then stopping the one and removing the other, either 'allow the patient to die' or 'kill the patient' depending on sensibility. Like the prayers affected by the maid's dropped pot, that process (even the salt's dissolution on the tongue is a process) which had maintained the patient's life has been interrupted and the patient dies. How would this be *essentially* different from disconnecting a moribund patient's oxygen line?

Interference with an oxygen *line* suggests by itself the fact that technology has made the distinction between active and passive euthanasia exceedingly dubious. Once, one might have argued that not bringing a cylinder of oxygen into the hospital room of a dying patient suffering intractable pain and thus allowing that patient to die was an act of *passive* euthanasia; one simply did nothing; *shev v'al ta'aseh*. Nowadays, the patient is connected by tubing to the oxygen pipes which are in the walls of the hospital room; to disconnect the tubing, one has to do something and that is *active* euthanasia, *kum v'aseh*!

One wonders whether much of the discussion about the two are distinctions without differences, particularly, if one deals with the question of motivation.If one intends to end the suffering of the moribund patient, whether in earlier times, by not bringing in the oxygen or in present times, by disconnecting the oxygen line, one has *intended* the same thing. The acting or not acting is a function of technology, not morality.

One could do nothing! This the advice of some decisors.[22] However, something *is* being done, if only to keep the patient alive! Even if the patient says, "Leave me be and do not give me any aid because for me death is preferable," according to one authority, "everything possible must be done on behalf of the patient".[23] "On behalf of the patient?" One wonders. Those who were guilty of capital crimes and who were condemned to die by the *arba mitot bet din*, the means of judicial execution, for them the *Gemara* prescribed a *mitah yafa* and Rashi explained the term as *sheyamut maher* and now for this suffering person, innocent of any capital crime, we are to do everything to keep him alive and do nothing to help him, *sheyamut maher*? For the one, a *mitah yafah* and for the other...? That does not seem to be the logic of *kal vahomer* that might apply nor does it seem to be the acting out of *v'ahavta l're'akha kamokha*! Is that what is meant by "everything possible [being]...done on behalf of the patient"?!

I think that the issue of euthanasia must be re-thought. For us as Liberal Jews, texts of the past have votes but not vetoes; however, the texts adduced, as we have seen, do not vote for what people have said they vote for. We face medical technologies which can make the process of *gesisah* not the seventy-two hour process known to the *halakhah* but a far more extended period. We have technologies that can deal with pain, but not all pain and not some pain over an extended period. Euthanasia, I said at the beginning of this paper, arises because of the connection of death, death which seems certain, and pain that seems uncontrollable.

To do nothing may mean to allow someone to suffer, not because there is a hope of recovery, but because we are unwilling to do something or perhaps because we think that suffering (for someone else, one must honestly say) is preferable to death.[24]

To do something? What is it that we should do? I would suggest that before we begin our rethinking - and I would like to present some preliminary thoughts, we deal with two bugaboos, the first, the so-called "slippery slope" argument and the second, the charge that somehow euthanasia, however accomplished and for whatever reason, is "murder".

The "slippery slope" suggests that if somehow we countenance

20

euthanasia, whether passive or active, we shall soon end up killing others who may be unwanted for physical or other reasons. One could as well argue that since Judaism accepted the death penalty and war, it allowed murder. Any complex ethical decision requires a balancing of goods. *Balancing* suggests the counterposing of values and options which if standing alone might be rejected. Hence such decisions require a ride on "the slippery slope". It is where one stops, that makes the difference.

There may or may not be distinctions between active and passive euthanasia;[25] there are certainly distinctions between different kinds of killing. Unless one is an absolute pacifist for whom all killing is wrong, we normally distinguish between killing in war, killing in self-defense, judicial executions, and murder. What we call 'murder' is a particular kind of killing, for the benefit somehow of the perpetrator and hardly for the benefit of the victim! Euthanasia, the *mitah yafah*, which deals with the patient whose condition is clearly terminal and who is suffering intractable pain, whether one agrees with the notion or not, *is* for the benefit of the victim. I would therefore argue that it hardly could be, as one has said, "plain murder". [26]

I would like to offer these thoughts on euthanasia as more of a meditation than a statement. I would like to take the phrase *mitah yafah* with Rashi's explanation *sheyamut maher* as a kind of rubric. Euthanasia, the *mita yafah*, for me, is an option only in the case of someone who is terminal, *sheyamut*, that he will die and that he not suffer further, we think of *maher*-speedily. Euthansasia,we have said applies to one who is in process of dying and who is suffering; we must be sure of the first and unable to control the second. (Those strictures should obviate many problems). If that person be lucid and not wish the battle for life to continue, then his/her wishes should be followed as to when and how the end should come,whether that end comes by not doing something or by doing something. If the patient be lucid, only she/he can make the determination [and here I would differ with Rabbi's maid !] If, however, the patient not be lucid, then if he or she has left some instrument to indicate his/her intentions, a "living will" or a letter to the physician, then those instructions should be followed. If the patient not be lucid and has left no instructions, then whatever the family and the physician acting for the patient must decide should be done. One would hope that they would be as kind as Hananiah's executioner and as concerned as Rabbi's maid.

With what we have suggested, we not gone as far as Rabbi's Yose's advice to the old lady. We have gone further than many a handbook on Jewish medical ethics would prescribe. We have done so, we think, because of the injunction *veahavta l're'akha kamokha* and because we think it to be ethical and 'Jewish' to limit pain for that person whose life is coming to an end in any case.

Notes

1. *Funk and Wagnalls Standard Dictionary of the English Language*, International Edition, Vol. I, p. 439.

2. *b. San* 45a. J. David Bleich seems to be alluding to this passage when he writes,"Elimination of pain is certainly a legitimate and laudable goal...it is certainly mandated by virtue of the commandment 'Love thy neighbor as thyself'" in Bleich, J. D., *Judaism and Healing: Halakhic Perspectives*, New York, 1981, p. 137.

3. Abraham, Abraham S. *The Comprehensive Guide to Medical Halachah*, Jerusalem and New York, 1990, p. 177.

4. Jakobovitz, Immanuel, *Jewish Medical Ethics*, New York, 1959, p. 123. We shall return to the term "active euthansia" as well as to some reflections on the notion that the patient "is already known to be on his deathbed."

5. Vishlitzky, L., *Madrich Refui L'fe Ha-Masoret Hayehudit*, Jerusalem, 1977, pp. 85, 86.

6. Rosner, Fred, *Modern Medicine and Jewish Ethics*, Hoboken, 1991, pp. 211, 212. It should be noted that the term "homicide" has different meanings than the term "murder."

7. Vislitzky, *Loc. cit.,* p. 86.

8..Rabbi's dates are given either as 135-193 C.E. or 135-c.220 C.E. Cf Strack, H.L. *Introduction to Talmud and Midrash*, New York, 1965, p. 118.

9. b. *Avodah Zarah* 18a. Translation mine. It will be noted that Rabbi Jehudah Ha-Nasi will play a part in the text dealing with euthansia. The manner of his death will present some issues for discussion.

10. E.g., Vizlitzki, *Op. Cit.*, p. 87; Rosner, *Op. Cit.*, p. 206.

11. *Tosafot, ad locum*, suggests the exception to such an injunction: if one feared that by unbearable tortures, idolators might force him to commit transgressions, it would then be licit, a *mitzvah* to harm oneself. He gives the example (*b. Gittin* 57b) of the children, boys and girls, taken to Rome for a life of "shame" who threw themselves into the sea. It should be noted that this exception has a number of interesting elements: the individual *fears* his inability to withstand that which is in the future; he/she is not *presently* suffering. Neither the boys or the girls in this tragic story had at the moment of their death suffered torture nor had they experienced the degradation of the life of "shame"; they died because of what they *anticipated*! Anticipated suffering, one might have deduced, is reason enough for suicide! Such a conclusion, to say the least, was not drawn.

12. That this story of Hananiah has two conflicting elements was noted by David Gordis in "The Ethical in Jewish Bio-Ethics", *Judaism*, Vol. 38, 1989, pp. 28-40. Gordis wrote, "The most obvious objection to reading this narrative (*b. Avodah Zarah* 18a) as a rabbinic endorsement of distinguishing between active and passive euthanasia is the reported behavior of Rabbi Hananiah himself. After all, is it so clear that his merely opening his mouth constitutes something along the lines of active euthanasia, while the contract with the executioner is passive?"

13. To use Rosner's gloss on the passage. Rosner, *Op. Cit.*, p. 206.

14. *b. Ketubot* 104a. Rashi *ad locum* explains that Rabbi was suffering from an intestinal complaint.

15. About Rabbi's maid, Rosner wrote, "This woman is reported to have prayed for his death" in *Jewish Bio-Ethics*, 1979, p. 271. He omits mentioning the fact that she "is reported" to have acted! Dr Bleich writes that the maid "...is depicted in rabbinic writings as a woman of exemplary piety and moral character. This woman is reported to have prayed for his death" , *Op. Cit.* ,p.142. He also omits mentioning that she did more than pray, she acted. He does note that after she"... expressed her feelings and conveyed information regarding her master's pain and discomfort to his disciples, they not only declined to join her in prayer for his decease, but did not desist from praying for the prolongation of his life." *Op.Cit.* p. 143. It is instructive to note what Drs. Bleich and Rosner extract and fail to extract from the passage; indeed, Dr. Bleich's grasp of detail is significant for what it omits.

16. Jacobovitz, *Op. Cit.*, p. 275.

17. *Yalkut Shimoni*,with introduction by Bezalel Landoy, Jerusalem, 1960, Vol II, Section 943, p. 980. The passage continues, "Therefore, Solomon said, 'Happy is the man who hearkens to me' (Pr. 8:34) [the point being the continuation of the verse: 'Watching daily at my gates,Waiting at the post of my doors']. What is written after that? 'He who finds me, finds life.' (Pr. 8:35). The continuation of the first verse and the second verse quoted suggest that attendance at the synagogue is a means of preserving life. If so, not going to the synagogue would be a way of ending one's life!

18. According to Bleich, *Op. Cit.*, p. 141, "...any patient who may reasonably be deemed capable of potential survival for a period of seventy-two hours cannot be considered a *goses.*" So here too, *time* becomes a factor of determining status.One wonders where the issue of euthanasia would ever arise were it clear that the moribund patient would live only seventy-two hours. If the "...Halakhah assumes axiomatically that the death process or 'the act of dying' cannot be longer than seventy-two hours in duration", Bleich, *ibid.*, then one can see why Bleich can say that "there is no obligation to perform any action to lengthen the life of a patient in this state" *Op. Cit.*, p. 140. Since the process has begun, one should neither advance or impede it.

19. *b. Semahot* Chapter One. This translation is taken from *The Minor Tractates of the Talmud*, London, 1965, Vol.I, pp. 326, 327.

20. Isserles, gloss on the *Shulhan Arukh, Yoreh Deah* 339, as quoted in Rosner, *Op. Cit.*, p. 207.

21. Rosner, *Op. Cit.* p. 198, writes: "Passive euthanasia is defined as the situation in which therapy is withheld so that death is hastened by omission of treatment. "There is no *omission* of treatment in Isserles' examples of the removal of impediments to death. Rosner also , *Op. Cit.*, p. 208, notes that "...the discontinuation of life-support systems which are specifically designed and utilized in the treatment of incurably ill patients might only be permissible if one is certain that in doing so one is shortening the act of dying and not interrupting life." The distinction between "the act of dying" and "life" seems to be the difference between seventy-two hours and a more extended period in the patient's life. Even so, Rosner seems to be suggesting more flexibility than other writers.One is reminded of a line in a speech given in an euthanasia debate in the House of Lords,"...the good doctor is aware of the difference between prolonging life and prolonging the act of dying" in Williams, Glanville, *The Sanctity of Life and the Criminal Law*, New York, 1968, pp. 336, 337.

22. Rosner, *Op. Cit.*, p. 210.

23. *Tzitz Eliezer*, IX, No. 47, Sec.5, quoted in Bleich, *Op. Cit.*, p. 137 and in Rosner, *Op. Cit*, pp. 210, 211.

24. Thus Dr Bleich, after mentioning the case of the guilty *sotah* who suffered in a "...debilitating and degenerative state, which led to a protracted termination of life," deduces from that case that "Life accompanied by pain is thus viewed as preferable to death." Bleich, *Op. Cit.*, pp. 135, 136.

25. James Rachel in his article "Active and Passive Euthanasia", *Contemporary Issues in Bioethics*, Beauchamp and Walters eds., Belmont, 1982, pp. 313-316, argues that there is no valid distinction between active and passive euthanasia, saying "...there is really no moral difference between the two, considered in themselves (there may be important moral differences in some cases in their *consequences*, but...these differences may make active euthanasia, and not passive euthanasia, the morally preferable option.)"

26. Jacobovits, Immanuel quoted in Rosner, *Op. Cit.*, p. 208.

SUICIDE, ASSISTED SUICIDE, ACTIVE EUTHANASIA
A *Halakhic* Inquiry

Peter Knobel

This paper deals with an excruciatingly difficult moral problem, the circumstances under which killing is permitted and who may terminate a human life.[1] Framed slightly differently, we have the following issues: In the case of a terminally ill person or one who is suffering severe and unremitting pain, would suicide, assisted suicide or voluntary active euthanasia be morally permissible? If so, under what circumstances?[2] The question has more than theoretical interest. Our acts and attitudes will help shape the social matrix of ethical decision making. Our goal is to give advice to Jewish ethicists, health care professionals, patients and their loved ones. In matters of life and death we must exhibit care that we do not undermine precisely the values we hope to support, namely the dignity and sanctity of human life.[3]

While speaking in general terms, it is essential to remember that our subjects are real people and the decisions that they must make about their lives, those they love and those for whom they care. In challenging established societal norms which seek to protect individual human life, one could begin a process which radically alters the way in which society treats the weak and the vulnerable.[4] If we propose an attitudinal shift in the "hard cases" do we change the attitude of individuals and society so as to encourage suicide and lead from a situation where people willingly waive their right not to be killed, under severely limited circumstances, to involuntary active euthanasia based on social worth?.[5]

Even naming the action has moral weight. Is suicide the moral equivalent of self-murder, or self-delivery, or voluntary ? Is assisted suicide the moral equivalent of being an accomplice to murder, or being an agent of compassion who assists in voluntary death? Is voluntary active euthanasia the equivalent of murder or is it justifiable homicide?[6]

Since this is meant to be a *halakhic* discussion, it is important to ask what texts may be legitimately used to inform the discussion? Phrased slightly differently, the question is what counts as part of the canon?[7] For this conversation I have utilized not only specifically Jewish texts but the work of ethicists some of whom are Jewish and whose approach has a specific Jewish flavor. In addition I have used ethicists and philosophers who were either secular or Christian to see in what ways they advanced the conversation. An important element that is missing in this paper and in many similar discussion is the woman's voice.[8] Feminist scholars suggest - and I concur - that we must pay much closer to the stories of individual people's lives and not just abstract principles. In deciding what is permissible to do and what is prohibited we must become good listeners. The texts that count are not only the written texts of our traditional or modern literature, but the texts and contexts of people's life. An important aspect of responsa is the fact that they are case specific and in large measure are concerned with the details of an individual case.

METHODOLOGY

It is now a truism in bio-ethical literature to say that beginning and end of life issues present us with some of the most difficult ethical dilemmas. New technologies are causing us to rethink the definitions of life and death and what constitutes medical treatment. Our ability to intervene in the process of conception and fetal development with *in utero* surgery and genetic engineering, and our ability to prolong life and death with medications and mechanical devices are the blessing and curse of modern medicine. These developments require a fundamental review of the way in which we make determinations.

Methodology often determines outcome.[9] A liberal *halakhic* approach is more than an attempt to look for lenient precedents within the law. It is essentially an ethical analysis of the structure of Jewish living.[10] Professor David Ellenson in an important article,[11] has identified two methodologies for making "moral choices" -- *halakhic* formalism and covenantal ethics.

Halakhic formalism "seeks to identify precedents from the rich literature of rabbinic Judaism in order to extrapolate principles and norms that would yield authentic Jewish prescriptions on specific issues...Viewed in this way, Jewish medical ethics evidence the same methodological concerns and qualities that one would discover in any legal process."

> This process as David A. J. Richards has observed displays two major characteristics. The first is that the judge, or the rabbi in our case, "infers from the legal standards applicable to a particular situation, from a body of so-called primary authority. In Jewish law this "body of so called primary authority" includes the Bible and the Talmud which assumes a "statutory" role in the Jewish legal system, and an ongoing process of judicial opinions contained in the responsa and codes that function in a "precedential" way. Here the interpretation of the law offered in the previous case (its holding) is seen to have a bearing on the adjudication of a contemporary case that deals, in the rabbi's opinion, with the same issue of law. A second feature of legal reasoning, related to, but not identical with the first, is that of "reasoning by analogy." Rabbis, in this instance, not only take prior holdings on a comparable issue into account when rendering their decisions, but extend "principles of law found applicable to some set of fact patterns... to other fact patterns which are in relevant respects similar."[12]

Ellenson concludes that the method is "relatively straightforward" and involves "plumbing the depths of Jewish law and discovering there the resources to resolve a perplexing moral issues."[13] *Halakhic* formalism begins by identifying precedents from the literature of classic Judaism in order discover the principles that describe the Jewish norms which apply to a particular situation. Where the foundational law (Bible,

29

Talmud), the statutory (Codes) and case law (Responsa) are clear the rabbis apply the texts and precedents to the current case in order to arrive at a legal decision. Where the rabbis are faced with situations without precedent in Jewish law, they seek to find within the law, principles which will allow them to draw a proper analogy from one set of circumstances to a very different set of circumstances. It is important to recognize that "The [rabbis]{in this system} are juxtaposing 'the particulars of [their] own case and various *halakhic* precedents and principles, thereby decid[ing] in which category [their] own case falls. Then they must apply these precedents and principles to the situation at hand.'" He warns that similarity of method does not preclude pluralism of response. The precedents can be applied leniently or stringently and there can be disagreement about relevance of precedents in any particular case. "Affirmation of a common methodology in no way ensures a single substantive outcome."[14]

Ethics refers to the standard or yardstick, the general principles we use in making our decisions. Ethics asks the question: What is the morally correct thing to do in any particular situation? Law answers a different question: what is permitted or prohibited by a particular society and what is a person's liability for punishment. Law defines the limits of proper conduct for a citizen of a particular society. Laws may be just or unjust, ethical or unethical. In fact, there are many areas of law where ethics is not a relevant consideration. An ideal society seeks to construct a legal system based on concepts of justice and fairness. In other words, a just society seeks to construct an ethical legal system. If Reform is to recover *halakhah* and to use an *halakhic* method it will need to be one which makes ethics central.

It is important to distinguish our way of interpreting *halakhah* from the traditionalists for a number of reasons, but most notably because we do not share the ideological assumptions which undergird their mode of thought and reasoning.[15] According to the traditionalists, *halakhah* is a system of law that is revealed by God and, therefore, what the *halakhah* prescribes or proscribes is ethical[16] because it is commanded by God. Since it is commanded by God its obedience is obligatory. The *halakhah* is ideally a crystallization of Jewish ethics. However, we Reform Jews have rejected the authority of the *halakhah*, in part because we deny its divine origin, and in part because as a system it has failed to respond adequately to modernity, the Enlightenment, and emancipation, and the rapid changes brought about by the technological revolution. We have frequently offered a moral critique of the *halakhah*. Its treatment of women is a prime example. In addition the *Shoah* (the Holocaust) and the rebirth of the state of Israel, have put strains on the traditional *halakhic* system. One reason for stagnation in the *halakhic* process is that the *halakhah* is a legal system lacking a legislative process.

A way to renew the *halakhic* process within a liberal context must begin by an explicit delineation of the methodological assumptions which undergird our work. David Ellenson's identification of "covenantal ethics" is a productive starting point. This method also cuts across denominational lines. Eugene Borowitz, a major Reform theologian, and Yitz Greenberg, a liberal Orthodox thinker, and Rabbi Daniel Gordis, a professor at the University of Judaism (Conservative), have made beginnings at spelling out this method. Among the principles which define this method are the following: One begins by examining Jewish texts to discover what it means to be human and the nature of humankind's relationship to God. Gordis calls this a theological anthropology. Humankind is both created in the image of God and serves as God's partner in the ongoing work of creation. This relationship of partnership is called *brit* or covenant and it entails obligations (*mitzvot*). The covenant is a loving relationship which may be described using the language of marriage. In such a loving relationship human freedom is not overwhelmed by divine will. Such a relationship is characterized by mutuality and respect for the integrity of each partner.[17] It is the dialogue and dialectic of the relationship which enables a person to become more fully human by recognizing the absolute worth of his/her personhood because it is in the image of the divine. In this model the

31

experience of God is genuine and revelation is genuine, but for the liberal Jewish thinker - following the model of Buber - only the ground of Jewish duty is revealed i.e., the presence of God. In the I-Thou moments of our personal and communal lives we experience the divine presence. From the intimacy of the relationship we intuit what is required of us.[18] The specifics of Jewish duty (*mitzvot*) are the human response to the experience of the divine. Yitz Greenberg adds that in our partnership with God we are encouraged to become more like God by mastering our environment. Further, the covenantal model takes Jewish tradition seriously, because the religious classics of Judaism are the accumulated wisdom of the Jewish people, which are authoritative by virtue of their testifying to the genuine struggle of the Jewish people to live within the covenantal relationship. To utilize the texts is to take one's stance as part of the continuing drama of Jewish history. It offers a specific locus for our being by placing us within a community. Our autonomy is limited by our willingness to bring our individual will under the scrutiny of collective wisdom and collective responsibility. It means we do not have to invent our Jewish selves nor do we exist in a lonely vacuum, but we are part of living community. With this method individuals have the right to exercise a great deal of control over their own lives. In such a system quality of life questions become are as valid as quantity of life questions.

Finally a system of covenantal ethics must also have a concept of a just society. Central to the formulation of such a concept are the historic experiences of the Jewish people as slaves in Egypt. Our tradition constantly calls upon us to identify with the weak and the powerless so that they may be liberated from the economic, social, political, and spiritual fetters which prevent their fully becoming *b'tzelem elohim* (in the image of God).[19] The *Shoah* also creates a moral imperative to prevent the dark forces which reside within the human soul from overwhelming our divine potential.[20] The *Shoah* is a warning which cannot be ignored. Jewish and human life become all the more sacred when faced with the smoking ovens. Further, the re-establishment of the State of Israel raises the hope that a renewed *halakhah* can yet establish a state infused with a covenantal ethics of human worth, justice and peace.[21]

Finally the *halakhic* formalists make the rabbi-decisor the ultimate judge of what is ethical and unethical. Within the covenantal model the rabbi serves as advisor and not decisor. Our model is one of shared decision making. The final arbiter is to use Borowitz's rich phrase, "the Jewish autonomous self" where self, tradition and community have been allowed to interact.

Elliot Dorff, in a significant paper on the central issues raised by this paper,[22] specifically rejects the covenantal method as a way of making *halakhic* decisions. He writes:

> Nevertheless I think that this approach is wrong headed. My view ultimately rests upon three factors: (a) my appreciation of the *strengths* of a legal approach to the moral issues in life and the corresponding weakness of the suggested alternative: (b) my conviction that personal responsibility can be retained in a properly understood *halakhic* system; and (c) my confidence that *when properly understood,* legal methods can enable Jewish law to treat realities as new as contemporary medical phenomena.

At least from a Reform theological perspective, which desires to re-invest the tradition with authority, a new understanding of our reading of the texts is necessary. Only then we will be able to offer advice that is clearly derived from a coherent reading of the tradition.

While a case can be made that in Reform responsa we follow the *halakhic* formalist method, I wish to argue that it is the covenantal method that we implicitly use and we should consider it the normative method for Reform *halakhic* decisions. Its advantage is to proceed from a Reform Jewish understanding of what it means to be human and the appropriate role of the individual in decision making. Clarification of these prior issues will determine what precedents in Jewish law will be given priority.

HUMAN DIGNITY AND THE SANCTITY OF HUMAN LIFE

Having set out a methodological framework, I wish to proceed with a consideration of the permissibility of suicide, assisted suicide and active voluntary euthanasia within a covenantal reflection on *halakhah*. This paper challenges the prevailing *halakhic* opinion opposing suicide, assisted suicide and active voluntary euthanasia.[23] It is my conclusion that under certain conditions, with appropriate safeguards, terminally ill patients[24] can morally take their own life, be aided to take their own life, or waive their right not to be killed. The doctrine of the sanctity of human life is rooted theologically in the concept that humankind was created *b'tzelem elohim* (in the image of God). Human dignity and worth are connected to the concept of *imitateo Dei* and biological life may be forfeited for good and sufficient reasons.[25]

For example, Maimonides identifies humankind's uniqueness and the God-like quality as residing in the superior intelligence of the human soul:

> The vital principle of all flesh is the form which God has given it. The superior intelligence in the human soul is the specific form of the mentally normal human being. To this form the Torah refers in the text, "Let us make a human being in Our image and after Our likeness" (Gen.1:26). This means that the human being should have a form that knows ... Nor does (this) refer to the vital principle in every animal by which it eats drinks, reproduces, feels and broods. It is the intellect which is the human soul's specific form. And to this specific form of the soul the Scripture phrase "In Our image, after Our likeness" alludes.[26]

Rabbi Irving Greenberg, a leading modern Orthodox thinker, whom David Ellenson identifies with the covenantal method, writing specifically in a bio-ethical context, defines the covenantal model using the metaphor of the partnership model. It is a partnership in the perfection of the world which takes seriously human value and dignity. Human freedom is real and not illusory. Greenberg emphasizes the human power working in concert with God to perfect the world. The greater the patient's say in those matters which affect the patient's life, the more God-like is the patient.[27] Using Genesis 1 and 3 Leon Kass, a leading bio-ethicist, argues:

> Man has special standing because he shares in reason, freedom, judgment, and moral concern, and, as a result lives a life freighted with moral self-consciousness. Speech and freedom are used among other things to promulgate moral rules and to pass moral judgments, first among which is that murder is to be punished in kind because it violates the dignity of such a moral being. We note a crucial implication. To put it simply, the *sanctity* of human life rests absolutely on the *dignity* - the god-like-ness - of human beings.[28]

Ronald Dworkin a leading legal theorist writes:

> The life of a single human organism commands respect and protection, then, no matter in what form or shape, because of the complex creative investment it represents and because of our wonder at the divine or evolutionary processes that produce new lives from old ones, at the processes of nation and community and language through which a human being will come to absorb and continue hundreds of generations of culture and forms of life and value, and finally, when mental life has begun and flourishes, at the process of internal personal creation and judgment by which a person will make and remake

himself, a mysterious inescapable process in which we will each participate and which is therefore the most powerful and inevitable source of empathy and communion we have with every other creature who faces the same frightening challenge. The horror we feel in the willful destruction of a human life reflects our shared inarticulate sense of the intrinsic importance of each of these dimensions of investment.[29]

Anyone who believes in the sanctity of human life believes that once a human life has begun it matters, intrinsically, that that life go well, that the investment it represents be realized rather than frustrated. Someone's convictions about his own critical interests are opinions about what it means for his *own* human life to go well, and these convictions can therefore best be understood as a special application of his general commitment to the sanctity of life. He is eager to make something of his own life, not simply to enjoy it; he treats his own life as something sacred for which *he* is responsible, something *he* must not waste. He thinks it intrinsically important that he live well, and with integrity....

Someone who thinks his own life would go worse if he lingered near death on a dozen machines for weeks or stayed biologically alive for years as a vegetable believes that he is showing more respect for the human contribution to the sanctity of his life if he makes arrangements in advance to avoid that, and that others show more respect for his life if they avoid it for him. We cannot sensibly argue that he must sacrifice his own interests out of respect for the inviolability of human life. That begs the question, because he thinks dying is the best way to respect that value. So the appeal to the sanctity of life raises here the same crucial political and

36

constitutional issues that it raises about abortion. Once again the critical questions is whether a decent society will choose coercion or responsibility, whether it will seek to impose a collective judgment on matters of the most profound spiritual character on everyone, or whether it will allow and ask its citizens to make the most central personality-defining judgments about their own lives for themselves.[30]

In contrast Leon Kass, in opposing the right of people to choose to kill themselves or to be killed, recognizes the "indignities and dehumanizations" that modern medical technology often imposes on the end of life and agrees that they ought to be removed. But he further argues:

Dignity in the face of death cannot be given or conferred from the outside but requires a dignity of soul in the human being who faces it.... Dignity as predicable of all human beings... is ... to tie dignity to those distinctively human features of human animals, such as thought, image-making, the sense of beauty, freedom, friendship, and the moral life, and not the mere presence of life....Courage, moderation, righteousness and other human virtues are not solely confined to the few. Many of us strive for them with partial success, and still more of us do ourselves honor when we recognize and admire those people nobler and finer than ourselves... Adversity often brings out the best in a man; and often shows best what he is made of. Confronting our own death - or the deaths of our beloved ones - provides an opportunity for the exercise of our humanity, for the great and small alike. Death with dignity, in its most important sense, would mean a dignified attitude and virtuous conduct in the face of death.[31]

Kass' description of courage in the face of death is important but it represents only one of the choices that one can make. Judaism does not make a virtue of suffering. In the face of incalculable pain, grievous sin, or indignity, death is a possible or even preferred moral choice.[32]

Daniel B. Sinclair in his important book, *Tradition and the Biological Revolution*, after a careful study of the relevant *halakhic* material concludes:

> Jewish law does not adopt the notion of sanctity of human life, at least not in its strong form. This notion is, in fact, based upon a theological concept, namely the sacred awe engendered by the very experience of being alive.... In the Jewish tradition it is generally accepted that life in itself is not endowed with intrinsic holiness; rather, holiness is a state to be achieved by dint of sustained effort.[33]

Characteristic of the human dignity and sanctity of life, implicit in the concept of being created in the image of God, is a large measure of autonomy.[34] As mentioned earlier in the paper a more complete analysis of the concept of what it means to be human is necessary, however, the above cited passages provide a theological mood which offers a patient-centered model of medical care which requires shared decision-making.

PERMISSIBLE KILLING [35]

In Judaism individual human life is highly valued, but that is determined in a number of different ways. In Judaism there is a right to life, or it may be better stated, a right not to be killed. May this right be waived and if so under what conditions? The killing of an innocent at his/her own hands, or by others, is not strictly prohibited but neither is it permitted without good and sufficient reason.[36] Even a guilty life is taken only after the most rigorous of legal procedures.[37] If saving a single human life takes precedence over *Shabbat*[38] then taking a human life requires more that a casual reason. If saving one human life is equivalent to saving the whole world[39] and taking a human life is like destroying the whole world, extreme care must be taken if we are to approve positive actions to bring life to an end.

The medical technological revolution has changed both the definition of death and the way in which we think about it.[40]

> Death has dominion because it is not only the start of nothing but the end of everything, and how we think and talk about dying... shows how important it is that life end *appropriately,* that death keeps faith with the way we want to have lived. We cannot understand what death means to people - why some would rather be dead than existing permanently sedated or incompetent, why others would want to "fight on" even in terrible pain or even when they are unconscious and cannot savor the fight, why so few people think that whether they live or die once they fall permanently unconscious does not matter to them at all - we cannot understand any of this, or much else that people feel about death, unless we turn away from death for a while and back to life.[41]

It is the *aggadah*, the sacred narrative of a person's individual life, that plays a significant role. The responsa literature is composed of questions and answers about individual cases. While the responsa have precedential significance, and describe the specific conditions under which the decision has arisen, no two cases are identical and the specifics of a particular case under consideration are determinative. If this is true, then the *halakhah* ought to be a crystallization of the *aggadah*. A covenantal approach to *halakhic* decision-making must understand the spiritual biography of the individual.

The most recent arguments concerning the definition of death ask whether brain death criteria, as generally accepted in the medical profession, are adequate.[42] Some have argued that a persistent vegetative state constitutes death and, therefore, the removal of life support does not constitute killing. Robert M. Veatch, in a provocative article, raises significant questions about the "whole brain definition of death" and suggests a new definition of death which allows for individuals to choose their definition of death.[43]

In general, discussions of end stage medical care in Judaism have centered around the concept of the *goses,* the immediately dying patient i.e. moribund patients expected to die within 72 hours.[44] A *goses* is fully alive and nothing can be done to hasten death. Hastening the death of a *goses* is murder.[45] More recently Daniel Sinclair and Elliot Dorff have used the concept of the *terefah* as a category to discuss end stage medical care.

> The classical definition is provided by Maimonides in reaction to the exemption of the killer of a *terafah.* The person is not liable to capital punishment on the grounds that the victim is 'already dead'. Maimonides definition runs as follows:'It is know for certain that he had a fatal organic disease and physicians say that his disease is incurable by human agency and that he would have died of it even it he had not been killed in another way..[46]

It is clear that Maimonides places an incurably ill person into another category. In some sense that person's life is compromised and his/her death by human hands is not murder.

The fundamental concept in the definition of a human *terefah* is, therefore, the inevitability of death[47] in contrast to the *goses* who is alive in every respect. The person's biography therefore is crucial. Let us consider the case of the death of King Saul.[48] When mortally wounded in battle he requests that his armor-bearer kill him, but the

40

armor-bearer refuses. Saul and the armor-bearer commit suicide to prevent torture and humiliation by the Philistines. The Biblical text neither condemns Saul nor his armor-bearer. While some of the subsequent rabbinic discussion argues that Saul, as king, is to be considered a special case; it is clear that his biography and person require an end with dignity. The act, in fact, preserves his dignity. Potential abuse seems to justify suicide. As we apply this to the question of the terminally ill, when continued medical care is no longer effective and there is no hope of recovery or even of amelioration, we must ask whether continued medical treatment does not constitute abuse or torture? It is Saul who initiates the request for help in killing himself. While this was a situation with no opportunity for reflection, we may correctly assume that Saul's decision was based on the fact that he was mortally wounded and that the maintenance of biological life was not in his best interest.

A second version of the story appears in II Samuel 1. [49] Here Saul is presented as too weak to kill himself and an Amalekite agrees to kill him, asserting that he could not have survived in any case. While David punishes the Amalekite for killing Saul, David's act seems to be more concerned with the political ramifications than the legitimacy of the act itself. This passage describes an act of active voluntary euthanasia. The Amalekite justifies his act both on the fact that Saul is dying and that Saul requests him to do so.[50] It is clear that the Amalekite believes he has done the correct thing.

While there is a general condemnation of suicide in Jewish tradition, it is permitted when continuing to live violates a fundamental principle of what life is all about. It is not only permitted but considered praiseworthy. Martyrdom is designated *qidush hashem* (sanctification of the divine name).

> On one occasion four hundred boys and girls were carried off for immoral purposes. They divined what they were wanted for and said to themselves, "If we

drown in the sea we shall attain the life of the future world." The eldest among them expounded the verse "The Lord said, I will bring again from Bashan, I will bring again from the depths of the sea" (Psalm 68:23). "I will bring again from Bashan" - from between the lion's teeth. "I will bring again from the depths of the sea" - those who drown in the sea. When the girls heard this they all leaped into the sea. The boys then drew the moral for themselves, saying, "If these for whom this is natural act so, shall not we for whom it is unnatural?" They also leaped into the sea. Of them the text says, "Yea, for thy sake we are killed all the day long; we are counted as sheep for the slaughter" (Psalm 44:23).[51]

Sidney Goldstein points out that "this passage contains some interesting problems.

1. Their possible involvement in sin was not immediate, i.e., no one was threatening or demanding that they do immoral acts at the moment they decided to take their lives.

2. They appeared to have some hesitation as to whether their act would be considered meritorious, as indicated by their discussion prior to their drowning themselves."[52]

They preferred death to a life which required them to live in a way which was inconsistent with their life plan. The prospect of being subject to conditions of torture and immorality justified their drastic act. In certain cases of unremitting pain and a terminal illness, which has diminished the person's ability to fulfill their understanding of what it means to be created in the image of God, an act of suicide or assisted suicide or active voluntary euthanasia would not only be permitted, but might be seen as praise-worthy. While one can admire the courage of one who struggles against pain and disability, there is also admiration for those who allow their deaths to make a statement about their lives. Knowing when the struggle is over takes great wisdom. The case of R. Hanniah b. Teradion is instructive.

> R. Hanniah b. Teradion was arrested by the Romans and, wrapped in a Torah, was burned at the stake. His disciples said: "Open you mouth so that the fire enters you." He replied, "Let Him who gave me [my soul] take it away, but no one should injure oneself." The executioner then said to him, "Rabbi, if I raise the flame and take away the tufts of wool from over your heart, will you cause me to enter into the life to come?" "Yes" he replied "then swear to me[he urged]." He swore to him. He thereupon raised the flame and removed the tufts of wool from over his heart, and his soul departed speedily. The Executioner then jumped and threw himself into the fire. And a *bat qol* exclaimed: "Rabbi Haninah b. Teradion and the Executioner have been assigned to the world to come." When Rabbi heard it he wept and said, "One may acquire eternal life in a single hour, another after many years."[53]

This passage has been subject to a great deal of analysis and is often used to demonstrate that active euthanasia is not permitted. What we have here is a situation of assisted suicide where the person is unable to act for certain emotional or moral reasons but is able to permit another to help him. The executioner is granted immediate eternal life for his act of mercy. In fact one can read this passage to suggest that relief of suffering which hastens death is not only permitted but meritorious, so meritorious that the executioner is immediately ushered into eternal life.

> On the day when Rabbi died the Rabbis decreed a public fast and offered prayers for heavenly mercy. They, furthermore, announced that whoever said that Rabbi was dead would be stabbed with a sword. Rabbi's

handmaid ascended the roof and prayed: "The immortals desire Rabbi [to join them] and the mortals desire Rabbi [to remain with them]; may it be the will [of God] that the mortals may overpower the immortals." When, however, she saw how often he resorted to the privy, painfully taking off his *tefillin* and putting them on again, she prayed: "May it be the will [of the Almighty] that the immortals may overpower the mortals." As the Rabbis incessantly continued their prayers for [heavenly] mercy she took up a jar and threw it down from the roof to the ground. [For a moment] they ceased praying and the soul of Rabbi departed to its eternal rest.[54]

This is also a famous and much discussed passage. The fact that it is *aggadic* and the fact that maid cared deeply for Rabbi makes it especially instructive. Careful analysis will show that she acted out of compassion, but in defiance of rabbinic prohibition. She comprehends that Rabbi's disciples had lost sight of their master's needs and were consumed with their own.[55] Their prayers were an extraordinary powerful artificial life support. In throwing the pot and interrupting the prayers she performed a positive act. In effect she killed him. There is a preference in Judaism and in general medical ethical literature to suggest that what makes her act morally acceptable is that it was indirect and she removed an impediment to dying rather than hastened his death.[56] Psychologically it is easier to deal with indirect rather than direct action and the concept of allowing to die has greater appeal than killing. The distinction is often difficult to maintain. The maid's act clearly terminated his life. There is not disapproval of the action. We should further note that the rabbis' prayers become a form of abuse and torture for while they kept him alive they no longer constituted therapy in any meaningful sense.

Sinclair in his analysis of the *terefah* comes to a noteworthy conclusion:

> It would appear that where the indirect termination of the life of a critically ill patient would result in the saving of a viable life, as is the case of organ transplants or the allocation of scarce medical resources Jewish law would, in principle, legitimate such an act, provided that an institutional framework existed for assessing the effect of such a deed upon the moral fabric of society and for administering discretionary punishments. In all cases involving the killing either directly or indirectly of a *terefah*, the killer would be exempt from the death penalty and his fate would be decided by extrajudicial bodies. These bodies would have at their disposal a whole range of sanctions, including death. Presumably, where proof was brought to the effect that the death of a *terefah* has been brought about in an indirect fashion for the sake of saving a viable life, those involved in the relevant acts would not be subject to any sanction.[57]

Sinclair's suggestion that killing be allowed for sake of *piquah nefesh* is very interesting. It means that he believes that one life can be sacrificed for the sake of another life. While he still wishes to maintain the distinction between direct and indirect means, the issue of intent is important.[58]

The Talmud,[59] in discussing capital punishment, uses Leviticus 19:18 "Love your neighbor as yourself" to argue that one should chose for the condemned criminal a *mitah yafah,* an easy death. Rashi defines a *mitah yafah* as a rapid death or one that does not humiliate the condemned. If we are to view condemned criminals as our neighbors and compassionately provide them with a rapid and non-humiliating death, what, then, is our obligation to innocent life which is suffering terrible pain and a humiliating death?[60]

INSTITUTIONAL AND SOCIETAL SAFEGUARDS

The model for modern medical care, as it is increasingly practiced and as it ought to exist ideally, is shared decision-making.[61] Patients have the right, in consultation with competent medical authorities, to determine their own course of treatment. In Judaism great weight is given to the preservation of health and seeking cures for illnesses and preserving life. Medical expertise is highly respect and is to be followed except for good and sufficient reasons.

Suicide represents a special problem because most suicides are depressed.[62] There are those who argue that there is no such thing as rational suicide. In addition, there is the legitimate concern that if permission is granted to terminally ill patients to commit suicide, others not terminally will be more likely to commit suicide or that people who are old and infirm will feel that they must "do the right thing" and take their own life. My plea with respect to suicide is that we place it in the category of "decriminalization" or, in *halakhic* terminology, placed into the category *lekhathilah - bediavad* (an act not valid in the first instance but valid after the fact). Decriminalization rather than legalization[63] is my preference. There is a difference between "may" and "should". I wish to maintain a negative presumption which must be overridden. We must maintain a strong preference for life over death. On the other hand, this will enable us to be more compassionate in our assessment of those who believe that their impending death should be a *mitah yafah* which Rashi defines as speedy with a minimum of humiliation. By rethinking our attitude we in fact might find that we are given an opportunity to explore the meaning of life and therefore of death with the terminally ill. If we are serious about self-determination as a characteristic of being *b'tzelem elohim,* then we must find ways to help make mortal choices in a considered way. Assisted suicide and voluntary active euthanasia require permission first from the person wishing to die and those who are expected to assist or perform the act. Therefore, they allow and require elaborate procedures to assure the act is consistent with one's understanding of the sacred quality of their personhood. One of the most difficult aspects of permitting acts of killing is to assure that they are in fact voluntary and in keeping with the total biography of the person. This requires the sustained involvement of a physician, who knows the patient well, consultation with family members and a rabbi, who has had serious conversations with the individual.[64] The patient's case needs to be presented to a panel of physicians who must agree on the medical facts involved and, from a Judaic perspective, a *Bet Din* should also be convened.[65] These are limitations on the autonomy or self-determination of the patient as there is also an important community interest in preserving life. The issues of informed consent and competence are very important.[66] Advance directives can play a significant role as they are supposed to instruct medical professionals and enable surrogate decision-making, and they would also constitute a part of the *aggadic* record which is essential to the covenantal approach. Such documents, in addition to the legal forms, ought to be like ethical wills which describe the person's most important values. It is our goal to provide a comprehensive picture based not just on persons as patients or when faced with a terminal illness but when they were best able to express themselves.

My suggestion has a number of common elements with the following procedure which Brock recommends before a patient would be allowed to terminate life or be assisted in the endeavor.

1. The patient should be provided with all relevant information about his or her medical condition, current prognosis, available alternative treatments and the prognosis of each.
2. Procedures should ensure the patients's request for euthanasia is enduring (a brief waiting period could be

required) and fully voluntary (an advocate for the patient might be appointed to ensure this).

3. All reasonable alternatives to improving the patient's quality of life and relieving any pain or suffering must have been explored.

4. A psychiatric evaluation should ensure that the patient's request is not the result of a treatable psychological impairment such as depression.[67]

CONCLUSIONS

Death is part of the meaning of life. How one dies ought to be consistent with how one lived one's life. In most case we do not have choices about the way we die. Judaism values the pursuit of health and the preservation of life as very important *mitzvot*. Arguments against capital punishment in Judaism exhibit an extreme theological resistance, even to the termination of the life of one who has committed a capital offense. Therefore, extreme caution must be taken that permission given in "hard cases" does not become a slippery slope through which people will be encouraged to "do the right thing" and terminate their lives or ask others to do it for them. However it is also clear in Judaism that biological life, while an important value, is not a supreme value which overrides all other considerations. Therefore, in extreme situations, the termination of human life is not considered a sin, but is in fact praiseworthy. The determining factor is whether the termination of life is consistent with the preservation of the person as a being created *b'tzelem elohim*. In other words, does the continuation of biological life violate the sacred character of the individual's life? Therefore, the *aggadah*, the sacred narrative of a person's life, becomes part of the *halakhic* decision-making process. Ideally the person, family, physician, and rabbi[68] will be involved in the initial decision. The decision would

48

be reviewed by impartial medical and rabbinic experts. The decision-making seems cumbersome, but is necessary to avoid conflict of interest and rash decisions. This might be a permissible limitation on autonomy.

For a terminally person in unremitting pain:

1. Suicide would be seen a morally permissible act when undertaken to preserve the sacred quality of a person's life, i.e. consistent with a person's biography. As noted above care must be taken to prevent suicide which is the result of temporary depression.
2. Assisted suicide is permitted when the decision is rational and can be demonstrated as consistent with the person's own biography.
3. Active voluntary euthanasia is permitted when the person has waived his/her right not to be killed and it is consistent with the person's biography.

Notes

1. The use of the term "killing" is deliberate. Avoiding euphemisms makes the moral seriousness of the issue clear.

2. By framing the question in this way my goal is to limit the parameters of the discussion to a single class of cases. However, this is no easy task because terms such as "terminally ill," "dying" or even "end stage medical care" have a certain ambiguity. It is beyond the scope of this paper to define these terms, but definitions are essential. While this essay is meant to be a general *halakhic* discussion of the issue of suicide, assisted suicide, and active voluntary euthanasia, actual decisions are made on a case by case basis. This is a theme to which I return in the body of the paper.

3. Arguments against sanctioning suicide, assisted suicide and active voluntary euthanasia invoke the concept of the "slippery slope" or the "wedge." Ethically one must always attempt to deal with unintended consequences. How does our desire to help an individual in a particular situation create circumstances that will harm others e.g. if we sanction suicide for a severely handicapped person who finds life intolerable, do we inadvertently pressure other handicapped persons to "do the right thing" and take their own lives? Do we not encourage society to consider them a burden rather than an ethical responsibility?

4. Jewish responsibility to the weak and the vulnerable in society is a significant focus of Torah legislation and prophetic critique of Israelite society. Rabbinic literature using the concept of *imitatio Dei*, emphasizes that the just society is one in which those who are weakest are protected, cared for and granted dignity. See the section "Foundation of Jewish Ethics" in *Contemporary Jewish Ethics* edited by Menachem Kellner New York, 1978 pp. 125-161. See Lev. 19:1 ff "Say to the congregation of Israel you shall be holy for I the Lord your God am holy." Deut. 10:18 "He executes justice for the fatherless and the widow, and loves the sojourner, giving him food and clothing. Deut. 24:19-21 "When you reap your harvest in your field, and have forgotten a sheaf in the field, you shall not go back to get it; it shall be for the sojourner, the fatherless, and the widow; that the Lord your God may bless you in all the work of your hands. When you beat your olive trees, you shall not go over the boughs again; it shall be for the sojourner, the fatherless, and the widow. When you gather the grapes of your vineyard, you shall not glean it afterward; it shall be for the sojourner, the fatherless, and the widow." Deut. 27:19 "Cursed be he who perverts the justice due to the sojourner, the fatherless, and the widow. And all the people shall say, Amen." Ps. 146:9 "The Lord watches over the sojourners, he upholds the widow and the fatherless; but the way of the wicked he brings to ruin." Jer. 22:3 "Thus says the Lord: Do justice and righteousness, and deliver from the hand of the oppressor him who has been robbed. And do no wrong or violence to the alien, the fatherless, and the widow, nor shed innocent blood in this place."

5. "First, the abortion parallel. In the 1960's, legalized abortion was proposed for the "hard cases," which were defined in different ways by different people. But, today, few can deny that, however defined, abortion is not limited to the "hard cases." In fact, rape, incest, gross genetic defect, and preservation of the mother's life make up less than 5% of the 1.5 million abortions performed annually in the United States. Rosenblum and Forsythe, "The Right to Assisted Suicide: Protection of Autonomy or an Open Door to Social Killing" *Issues in Law and Medicine*, Vol. 6 #1, 1990, 26. This journal has a very strong "right to life" orientation. However, the issue it raises is of real importance. A significant concern in the literature is the "slippery slope." In many ways this is the most difficult aspect of the issue to discuss. A central concern is not only the impact on individuals but on society as a whole. Does approval of suicide, assisted suicide or voluntary active euthanasia in certain specific, ethically justified, cases make the weak more vulnerable? Is our commitment to the sanctity of human life diminished when we condone the killing of innocent people? Is the connection between the *Shoah* and euthanasia so inexorable, that it makes any endorsement of "the right to die" a path to mass murder? Does the "rational" decision of a person to end his/her life translate into an obligation on the part of others to do the "right thing" and end their lives?

6. The ambiguities inherent in the terminology as well as the ethical situation are discussed by Joseph A. Edelheit "The Ambiguity of Suicide and the Right to Die" *Machshavot: A Journal of the Chicago Board of Rabbis* Summer 1992 pp.5-10. The historical analysis of suicide in Droge and Tabor's book *A Noble Death: Suicide and Martyrdom Among Christian and Jews in Antiquity* provides an understanding of how contemporary attitudes developed. Sidney Goldstein's work *Suicide in Rabbinic Literature* provides a detailed discussion of the *halakhic* attitude toward suicide.

7. I recognize that in fact they are two different questions. However, it is my belief, as will be discussed in the section on methodology, that the way in which we do *halakhah* must be broadened. Non-*halakhic* texts and general Jewish and philosophical ethical discussion should be given greater weight in creating a hermeneutic for reading *halakhic* texts.

8. Carol Gilligan *A Different Voice* Cambridge MA, 1982. Karen Lebacq "Feminism and Bioethics: An Overview" *Second Opinion*, Vol. XVII, #2 1991, pp. 11-27.

9. In another context see the very interesting debate between Craig Evans and Jacob Neusner on the nature of the Mishna and the role of the messianic speculation during Mishnaic times. Craig A. Evans "Mishna and Messiah 'in Context': Some Comments on Jacob Neusner Proposals: *JBL* Vol.112,#2 Summer, 1993 pp 267-289 and Jacob Neusner "The Mishna in Philosophical Context and Out of Canonical Bounds" *JBL* Vol. 112, #2 Summer 1993, pp. 281-304. Methodology is extremely important and often determinative. However, it is true that people using similar methodologies may come to different conclusions or that people using different methodologies may in fact arrive at similar if not identical conclusions. See Ellenson "How to Draw Moral Guidance from a Heritage: Jewish Approaches to Mortal Choices" in *The Ethics of Choice: A Time to be Born and a Time to Die*, ed. Barry S. Kogan, New York, 1991 pp. 219-32.

10. Harold Schulweis, "The Character of Halakhah Entering the Twenty-First Century" *Conservative Judaism*, Vol.XLV, #4 Summer, 1993, pp. 5-13, an appeal to the Conservative Movement calls for an ethical reflection on the *halakhic* process to redeem it from irrelevance.

11. Ellenson, *Op. Cit.*

12. Ellenson p. 221 citing David A. J. Richards, *The Moral Criticism of the Law*, Encino and Belmont, CA, 1977 p. 28.

13. *Ibid.* p.321.

14. *Ibid.*

15. Meta-*halakhic* issues are often ignored or explicitly denied by traditional decisors. In Reform *halakhah* the gap between traditional precedents and the final decision needs to be filled with analysis of why the meta-*halakhic* (read ethical) is essential to the determination of the decision. In Reform Judaism, we are hermeneutically bound to the principle that God cannot command the unethical. The issue of revelation is significant because our rejection of verbal revelation allows greater latitude both of method and substance yet it threatens the integrity of the systems as law. Guidance in strict sense is affirmable on the basis of wisdom and authenticity but governance is more difficult to affirm. But framing the issue in terms authority and autonomy is unproductive. The case for *halakhah* in Reform will be made on the basis of its ability to create a way to live a sanctified life which preserves the Jewish people and contributes to human dignity.

16. Reform Judaism operates with an ethic which is independent of the *halakhah* and functions as a hermeneutical device to critique the *halakhah*.

17. David Hartman *A Living Covenant: The Innovative Spirit in Traditional Judaism,* New York, 1985 pp. 272-273.

18. It is the relationship of the individual to the historical experience of the community which is crucial. Implied in being Jewish, is the connection to the covenant. The whole discussion is relevant only to someone who is willing to live within a covenantal framework.

19. These concepts are particularly important when making decisions about life and death. We are dealing with individuals each of whom is of infinite worth but we do not deal with them in isolation, for how we treat them reflects on the society as a whole.

20. Eugenics, euthanasia for mentally retarded, murder of homosexuals as preludes to the mass destruction of Jews serve as a warning. Some argue that these acts in and of themselves are sufficient to oppose assisted suicide or voluntary euthanasia. The "slippery slope" is too steep to risk the inevitable fall.

21. The potential for the full development of a judaically based law (I deliberately avoided the use of the word *halakhah* here for a number of reasons not germane to this paper.) in Israel is an exciting possibility fraught with many difficulties and significant questions. Some *halakhists* argue that certain acts would be permitted in a Jewish state operating with the Jewish understanding of the sacredness of human life which would not be permitted in non-Jewish societies where the protections against abuse are not as great. While I am not at all sure that this is true, it does again serve as a warning that if we permit the termination of life in some extreme circumstances, we may inadvertently diminish the protection of weak, vulnerable and innocent life.

22. Elliot N. Dorff "A Jewish Approach to End-Stage Medical Care", *Conservative Judaism,* Vol. XLIII, #3 Spring, 1991, p. 5. The *halakhic* method pursued in Elliot Dorff's paper has much in common with the covenantal method. I believe that in liberal *halakhic* circles the methods overlap either explicitly or implicitly.

23. The overwhelming opinion of *halakhic* authorities, Reform, Conservative, and Orthodox, opposes euthanasia whether in the form of suicide, assisted suicide, or physician initiated. The following statements from Reform responsa are representative. Israel Bettan in 1950 wrote, "The Jewish ideal of the sanctity of human life and the supreme value of the individual soul would suffer incalculable harm if, contrary to the moral law, men were at liberty to determine the conditions under which they might put an end to their own lives and the lives of other men." *American Reform Responsa* p. 263. A finer distinction between removing impediments rather than hastening death may be summarized in the statement of Solomon B. Freehof in 1969 " To Sum up: If the patient is a hopelessly dying patient, the physician has no duty to keep him alive a little longer. He is entitled

to die. If the physician attempts actively to hasten the death, that is against the ethics of Jewish law. In the case described, the term used in the question, 'hasten death,' is perhaps not correct, or at least should be modified. The physician is not really hastening death; he has simply ceased his efforts to delay it." *American Reform Responsa,* p. 260 Finally in a 1980 responsum Walter Jacob and the CCAR Responsa Committee state, "We would not endorse any positive steps leading toward death. We would recommend pain killing drugs which would ease the remaining days of a patient's life. We would reject any general endorsement of euthanasia, but where all 'independent life' has ceased and where the above mentioned criteria of death {sic. brain death} have been met further medical support systems need not be continued."

In a number of cases we may be dealing with a semantic difference between the concept of "doing" and "allowing to happen." A fundamental question remains, if we can relieve suffering for a terminally ill patient who is aware that this will kill him/her and grants permission is this an immoral act? Is there any moral difference between not starting a respirator or removing a respirator? Do we show greater respect for the sanctity of human life in permitting continued suffering or eliminating that suffering at the authorized request of the sufferer?

24. I have avoided offering a definition of terminal illness. For my purposes a terminal illness is one which inevitably lead to death and for which medical treatment has been exhausted. Progressive chronic diseases such as Alzheimer's disease raise important questions. They rob people of their personhood and their ability to function independently. Is dementia pain for the demented or only for those who love that person? I am particularly sensitive to people with AIDS.(See Yoel H. Kahn's sermon Choosing the Hour of Our Death" *CCAR Journal* forthcoming). I am opposed to involuntary euthanasia as a violation of the sanctity of human life. A person has a right not to be killed. That right might be waived. I am sympathetic to those, who faced with such a diagnosis, have chosen to end their life. However, the major thrust of this paper concerns those for whom death is certain and pain intractable. Pain management is an art and one at which physicians have become more adept which increasingly relieves the suffering of the dying. I believe the human will to survive and cling to life will limit the number of people who will choose death. However, choosing to die rather than suffer the loss of one's personhood can be a moral act.

25. As anyone who had studied both recent responsa and medical ethical literature knows the question of what constitutes biological life is much debated. Robert M. Veatch "The Impending Collapse of the Whole-Brain Definition of Death *Hasting Center Report* 23, #24, 1993, pp. 18-24. Fred Rosner *Modern Medicine and Jewish Ethics,* New York, 1986, pp. 241-254.

26. *Mishneh Torah, Hilkhot Yesodei Ha-Torah* 4:8 See Jacob Neusner, *The Glory of God is Intelligence*, Salt Lake City, 1978 p. 2ff.

27. Irving Greenberg, "Toward a Covenantal Ethic of Medicine" in Levi Meir, *Jewish Values in Bioethics*, New York, 1986, pp. 124-29.

28. Leon R. Kass "Death with Dignity and the Sanctity of life" *The Ethics of Choice A time to Be Born and A time To Die*, p. 128. Kass argues very strenuously here and in his "Is There a Right to Die?" *Hasting Center Report*, Vol. 23, #1, January-February, 1993, pp. 34-43, against the concept

that there is a right to die or that either assisted suicide or active voluntary euthanasia are permitted. See Ronald Greens response "Good Rules Have Good Reason: A Response to Leon Kass in *The Ethics of Choice A Time to Be Born and A Time To Die* pp. 147-56.

29. Ronald Dworkin, *Life's Dominions: An Argument about Abortion, Euthanasia and Individual Freedom*, New York, 1993 p. 84.

30. *Ibid.* 215-26 Similarly Dan W. Brock identifies self determination as a significant criterium for making mortal decisions. He defines self determination as "people's interest in making important decisions about their lives for themselves, according to their own values or conception of a good life, and being left free to act on those decisions. Self-determination is valuable because it permits people to form and live in accordance with their own conception of a good life at least within in the bounds of justice and consistent with others doing so as well." *Life and Death Philosophical Essays in Biomedical Ethics,* Cambridge, England, 1993, pp. 205-206

31. Leon Kass "Death with Dignity and the Sanctity of life", pp. 132-34.

32. See below.

33. Daniel B. Sinclair, *Tradition and the Biological Revolution,* Edinburgh, 1989, p. 81.

34. An interesting and frightening passage in *The Art Scroll Commentary* on Joshua, (ed. Reuven Drucker, Brooklyn, 1982) links the value of human life to the concept of creation in the divine image with behavior and not merely biological life. On one level the passage clearly supports the concept that biological life may be forfeited under certain circumstances and therefore rejects any absolutist concept of the sanctity of human life It raises a serious warning that when we either offer moral or other criteria which permit the killing of individuals (or in this case "nations") we come dangerously close to the "slippery slope."

> Since the Torah places infinite value on each individual by definition, the value of several persons cannot exceed the value of one. One infinity and one thousand infinities are equally large. Yet the *Book of Joshua* chronicles the wholesale slaughter of the Seven Canaanite Nations. How can the Torah countenance, let alone command such destruction of human life? How can this campaign of extermination be reconciled with the principle of sanctity of human life? The answer is that a life has value only insofar as it bears the imprint of the Divine. Man was created in the image of God and it is this *image* which confers value upon the substance of his body. If an individual is irrevocably entrenched in behavior which denies the very being and authority of the Divine he reverts to a mere clod of chemicals.

35. I wish to emphasis that the use of word "killing" is deliberate. We must always be aware of the moral seriousness of a decision to terminate human life. While Jewish law and many ethicists make a moral distinction between killing and allowing to die, I am convinced that first of all, in many cases, the distinction is not really clear, for example, the notion of double effect where one gives pain medication in sufficient doses to relieve pain but at the same time one actually hastens death. Since the intent was the relief of pain, not killing the patient, it is morally permissible, but giving a deliberately lethal dose of the pain-killer is ethically wrong. The concept of *shev v'al ta'aseh* (sit and do nothing) requires re-examination.

36. Abortion raises a number of the same issues. While the status of the fetus is not that of a *nefesh* "juridical person," it is clear that its status as a potential life is not morally trivial. Most authorities limit permissible abortion to cases where there are direct or indirect threats to the mother's life or health. Where authorities permit the abortion of a severely handicapped fetus, it is done for maternal reasons. It is the mother's quality of life which is at stake. Some liberal authorities have argued that a severely impaired fetus has a right not to be born. The danger of the slippery slope exists in these cases as well where perfection is seen as the ideal. How much handicap is sufficient to waive the fetus' right to be born? I always think about a wonderful young man in my congregation with Downs Syndrome who is one of the sweetest people I know and a young boy who is profoundly deaf. In spite of some limitations they bring great joy and beauty to the world.

37. Capital punishment is a case in point. It is clear that both the Torah and later rabbinic literature permit capital punishment. The judicial restrictions against enforcement, which develop mostly after Jewish courts no longer have the authority to impose capital punishment, make it clear that even killing a guilty person is not done without some moral reservations.

38. *M. Sanhedrin* 4:5

39. *B. Yoma 85a*; *Shabbat* 132a

40. Avram Reisner in his response to Elliot Dorff in describing natural death, indicates how far, in many cases today, we are from such a concept, and, therefore, places certain mechanical devices such as heart-lung machines, respirators, dialysis machines and some transfusions in the category of "impediments to dying". He, like most Jewish authorities, wants to maintain the ethical distinction between removing impediments to dying and killing. There is a danger here that such a way of thinking will in fact dilute the moral seriousness of these issues.

> What constitutes natural death? The cessation of the integrated biological functioning of an organism due to natural causes. Perhaps surprisingly, all deaths have one proximate cause - the deprivation of oxygen to the cells. The mechanisms that lead to a shortage of oxygen and the death of a cell may differ considerably, but whether the heart ceases to circulate the blood due to mechanical failure or whether the lungs cease to maintain the oxygen levels in the blood or whether either of these follow upon a breakdown of instructions from the brain stem (brain death as it must be defined by the

halakhah), the proximate cause remains the same. Yet not all deaths are the same in our moral accounting. We recognize some deaths as untimely, and others as natural.

Death by violence is culpable not because the death is intrinsically different from a natural death but because of the agent and the untimeliness. Death by famine and disease (not caused by specific human design) is intolerable but not culpable because the agent is "an act of God" but the death remains, in our minds, untimely. Death of old age is neither intolerable nor culpable since it is timely and attributable to the nature of our creation. The permission granted in the Torah for a physician to heal, according to the primary *midrash* of (*rapo yerape*) is, in the first instance, granted with regard to injuries in the first category. Of healing in the second category there existed some debate; perhaps these afflictions should be taken to be God's will, but Jewish law and tradition ruled firmly that here, too, we are required to act to the extent of our ability. The third category was never before susceptible to our ministrations. Nor is it evident that it should be or ever will be meaningfully within our ken. This, ultimately, is God's calculation. This, it seems to me, is the theological rationale behind removing impediments to death - and not primarily the relief from pain (which is the rationale behind praying for death). We try in all our dealings, including healing and including death, to act in that way which corresponds to God's will.

The diagnostic problem remains. How do we determine that a particular death is "natural" and timely, according to God's will and plan? The answer must reside within medicine.

If timely death - the ultimate death of God's choice - will not be meaningfully affected by our ministrations, we need only see if our medicine is able or futile. Here is the law of treatment of the dying rephrased. By doing everything possible medically, biologically, to treat the life systems of the critical patient, while removing impediments to death, items or procedures that interfere with the natural shut-down of the body's major systems in death, we allow ourselves to see if, indeed, God has ordained the closure of this life, while we do not cede at all our roles as healers and nurturants. Avram Israel Reisner "A Halakhic Ethic of Care for the Terminally Ill", *Conservative Judaism*, Vol. 43, #3, 1991 pp. 58-59.

41. Dworkin, *op. cit.* p.199.

42. Reform Judaism accepts brain death criteria, see Walter Jacob, "Euthanasia", *American Reform Responsa*, New York, 1983, p. 272. There is an ongoing argument in the Orthodox community See Fred Rosner, *Modern Medicine and Jewish Ethics*, Hoboken, 1986 pp. 241-254.

43. "An individual who has sustained irreversible loss of consciousness is dead. A determination of death must be made in accordance with acceptable medical standards. However, no individual shall be considered dead based on irreversible loss of consciousness if he or she, while competent, has explicitly asked to be pronounced dead based on irreversible cessation of all functions of the entire brain or based on irreversible cessation of circulatory and respiratory functions. Unless an individual has, while competent, selected one of these definitions of death, the legal guardian or next of kin (in that order) may do so. The definition selected by the individual legal guardian or next of kin shall serve as the definition of death for all legal purposes." Veatch, "The Impending Collapse of the Whole-Brain Definition of Death" *Hastings Center Report*, # 23, 1993, p.23.

44. See the discussions by both Dorff and Sinclair for all of the relevant citations and ethical distinctions.

45. A person on the deathbed (*goses*) is like the living in every regard.. One does not bind his cheeks or stop his orifices... Ones does not save him or wash him.. until the moment he dies. Whoever touches and moves him, that one commits murder. Rabbi Meir would compare him to a candle which is flickering; should a person touch it, it immediately goes out. (*Shukhan Arukh, Yoreh Deah* 339.1 as cited by Avram Israel Reisner "A Halakhic Ethics of Care for the Terminally Ill", *Conservative Judaism*, Vol. 40, #3, 1991, p. 56.

46. *Hilkhot Rozeah* 2.8; Sinclair *Op. Cit.* p.20

47. Sinclair *Op. Cit.* p.21.

48. I Samuel 31:1 Now the Philistines fought against Israel; and the men of Israel fled before the Philistines, and fell slain on Mount Gilbo'a. And the Philistines overtook Saul and his sons; and the Philistines slew Jonathan and Abin'adab and Mal'chishu'a, the sons of Saul. The battle pressed hard upon Saul, and the archers found him; and he was badly wounded by the archers. Then Saul said to his armor-bearer, "Draw your sword, and thrust me through with it, lest these uncircumcised come and thrust me through, and make sport of me. " But his armor-bearer would not; for he feared greatly. Therefore Saul took his own sword, and fell upon it. And when his armor-bearer saw that Saul was dead, he also fell upon his sword, and died with him. Thus Saul died, and his three sons, and his armor-bearer, and all his men, on the same day together. And when the men of Israel who were on the other side of the valley and those beyond the Jordan saw that the men of Israel had fled and that Saul and his sons were dead, they forsook their cities and fled; and the Philistines came and dwelt in them. On the morrow, when the Philistines came to strip the slain, they found Saul and his three sons fallen on Mount Gilbo'a. And they cut off his head, and stripped off his armor, and sent messengers throughout the land of the Philistines, to carry the good news to their idols and to the people. They put his armor in the temple of Ash'taroth; and they fastened his body to the wall of Beth-shan.

57

49. II Samuel 1:1-10 "After the death of Saul, when David had returned from the slaughter of the Amalekites, David remained two days in Ziklag; and on the third day, behold, a man came from Saul's camp, with his clothes rent and earth upon his head. And when he came to David, he fell to the ground and did obeisance. David said to him, Where do you come from? And he said to him, I have escaped from the camp of Israel. And David said to him, How did it go? Tell me. And he answered, The people have fled from the battle, and many of the people also have fallen and are dead; and Saul and his son Jonathan are also dead. Then David said to the young man who told him, How do you know that Saul and his son Jonathan are dead? And the young man who told him said, By chance I happened to be on Mount Gilboa; and there was Saul leaning upon his spear; and lo, the chariots and the horsemen were close upon him. And when he looked behind him, he saw me, and called to me. And I answered, Here I am. And he said to me, Who are you? I answered him, I am an Amalekite. And he said to me,' Stand beside me and slay me; for anguish has seized me, and yet my life still lingers. So I stood beside him, and slew him, because I was sure that he could not live after he had fallen; and I took the crown which was on his head and the armlet which was on his arm, and I have brought them here to my lord. "

50. See the discussion of Samuel Atlas, in Walter Jacob (ed.), *American Reform Responsa*, pp. 266-267.

51. *B. Gittin* 57b.

52. Sidney Goldstein, *Suicide in Rabbinic Literature,* New York, 1989. p. 43.

53. *B. Avodah Zarah* 18a-b.

54. *Ketubot* 104a.

55. The patients best interests take precedence over others when it comes to medical treatment.

56. There is good reason ethically to suggest in most cases that indirect acts or the removal of impediments is preferable. However, we are dealing with extremes and we are also dealing with situations where the distinctions are less clear, but the outcome is no less conclusive. The termination of human life is never morally trivial.

57. Sinclair *Op. Cit.* 62-63.

58. Brock argues convincingly that there is little distinction between killing and allowing to die. Intent is crucial. The same act or omission is moral or immoral depending upon intent. One who acts in the patients' best interests rather than his or her own has committed a moral act. One who acts in his/ her own interest commits an immoral act. Brock *Ibid.* pp. 162-65 Dorff *Ibid.* p. 15 argues that "we do nothing to hasten death and thereby co-opt the prerogative of God to determine such matters.." He maintains the distinction between sustaining life and prolonging death. The usual source of most Jewish medical ethicists is that Judaism permits only passive euthanasia defined as

58

removing impediments to dying.

59. *B. Sanhedrin* 45a and Rashi ad. loc.

60. It is essential for this paper that we are dealing with a competent patient who has either chosen to exercise his/her own right to die or has explicitly waived his/her right not to be killed.

61. *Ibid.* p. 55 ff. Dorff while arguing that "individual Jews do not, under Jewish law, have the same degree of autonomy they increasingly enjoy under American Law, ... nevertheless ... individual Jews do determine considerable elements of their health care." Dorff *Ibid.* p.12

62. This flies in the face of the traditional *halakhah* which defines "a culpable suicide, subject to *halakhic* penalties is one carried out through responsible choice, with intent definitely stated by the perpetrator and clearly understood by the listener." Goldstein *Ibid.* p.14

63. I recognize that there are significant problems with the terminology. My bias is not to allow, rather than to recommend, acts of killing in extreme situations.

64. This could either be the family rabbi - especially if he or she had ongoing involvement with the patient - or a specially trained rabbi. It would be advisable, in either case, that the rabbi have training in acquiring knowledge about an individual life plan. I believe that the skill necessary to elicit oral history would be important in this case.

65. Approval would, therefore, carry Judaic weight. The *Bet Din* would be in a position to weigh the Judaic considerations. This could have a powerful impact on this situation. I recognize a number of practical, psychological and potential legal difficulties.

66. Dan W. Brock has a detailed description of a model of informed consent and of shared decision making in his book *Life and Death* pp. 21-54, 55-79.

67. Brock *Ibid.* pp. 225-226.

68. Ideally these are all people who know and love this person who could be expected to support what is consistent with the person's biography and his/her best interests. However, checks and balances are required because of the seriousness and irreversibility of the decision.

RABBI JUDAH'S HANDMAID
Narrative Influence On Life's Important Decisions

William Cutter

Most of us know that revolutionary technical tools influence our bio-ethical decisions. Miraculous medical strategies have helped us redefine terms whose meaning we once understood like "draconian measures," "euthanasia," and "triage". Cessation of brain wave is replacing cessation of breathing as the principal criterion for when death has occurred. There is a consequent re-definition (for many *halakhic* Jews) of what constitutes a person who is in a dying state, a *goses*.[1] Social science categories have changed to an equally dramatic extent and some of our institutions and habits look surprisingly different: Families are redefined, old age does not mean what it used to mean, and medical care has moved out of the hospitals. Communitarian values have given way to the valorization of individual experience. And, finally, we have experienced a unique meeting of socio-economic and technological reality in a crashing irony: Our medical successes, people's expectations of cure, and our complex delivery systems have created a nearly intolerable economic burden for individuals and for society.

Both the technological and the sociological changes have added to our sense of uncertainty by creating a more dynamic and less anchored environment. Antidotes are always at hand, compensations for what is missing, new solutions to the new environments and their problems. This has been true even with regard to Jewish law, whose dynamism was both the goal and the means of thinkers like Solomon B. Freehof. Freehof's thinking with the passage of time has come to be an even stronger indication of the genius of Judaism to adapt. As Elliot Dorff has said: "Every legal system seeks to provide for both constancy and change."[2] In a world where change threatens stability, a certain talent for change can enhance it.[3]

Does every moment of life have infinite value? Or, Can ultimate values change along with intellectual method? J. David Bleich has insisted that every moment of life has infinite value, and is therefore indivisible. The idea that only the Creator can take away what has been given,[4] remains an inspired absolute that combats an ever-threatening sense of relativism. Yet we know that society at large may not be served by preserving life per se, no matter what Jewish norms encourage. We don't like to talk this way, but such ideas are on people's minds.

TRUTH CLAIMS VERSUS PRAGMATIC USE OF TEXTS

Obviously Orthodox Jews rely on the idea that Judaism can make truth claims, and can therefore require particular behavior from its adherents. While accommodation is inevitable, even for Orthodox Jews, it is rarely defended on purely pragmatic grounds. Different groups of Jews may have different justifications for accommodation. In a perspective of the middle ground, Dorff's position, for example, the argument is made that accommodation occurs comfortably within the legal system itself, and even Orthodoxy subscribes to the principle of *shinui itim*. Liberal thinkers struggle to make the claim of timeliness and viability, but sometimes wind up using methods that ill suit their inevitable conclusions. From a liberal perspective there are more purely utilitarian purposes attached to religious adherence. A liberal argument might contend that we need religious tradition and its prescriptions to preserve communitarian norms, and to remind us of the value of life under divine providence. But many liberal thinkers are probably willing to relinquish specific decisions to those who understand contemporary scientific empirical evidence. Their medical decisions are likely to determine the decisions of the modern liberal. While liberals may applaud certain absolutes in the interest of preserving a sense of traditional value and stability, these more nearly absolute norms probably will not be applied in the experience of the sick room unless they make scientific or economic sense.

In one way or another, when Jewish norms have loosened a bit, whether from a traditional or a liberal perspective, it is as a concession to technological reality, a reluctant submission to this or that new aspect of the environment: people live too long, living on a machine is not living, disease does not mean the same thing it used to, or our economy cannot handle extended illness in old age.

Yet these technological advances and social changes have not really had as much to do with changing the way we *think* about Jewish-bio-ethics.[5] Jews must find a way to link Jewish *ways of* thinking with technological progress - beyond finding a nexus for accommodation. This will be the task for the next generation of ethical thinkers, and my essay is a modest effort to nudge our thinking in that direction. It will do so by suggesting that we may be able to face more fully the realities with which we are living by applying new kinds of questions to medical ethics.

OLD FASHIONED RESPONSES TO TECHNOLOGY

Most people agree that the miracles of science have stretched our imaginations, and that the social experience of our people is vastly different from the experience of insulated communities in which much Jewish law developed. What I seek is a means of thinking that is more natural to human experience - moving towards an even more existential mode of thinking than is allowed by the current Jewish tendency to rely on case method for its flexibility. Case thinking tries to embrace technology, perhaps by applying a recent case based on an earlier principle to a case at hand. It incorporates technological reality into the discourse and permits a new variation on the original principle. For my work, however, I resort to one of the oldest pre-technological and pre-modern activities known to our civilization: The telling of stories. Story telling will be involved in this discussion in two ways: as a reflection of the real and lived experience of the patient in home or hospital; and as a cue to how we might make decisions regarding the last stages of a loved one's illness. In this second regard we must be nearly as rigorous with our use of stories as we have been with our application of "*halakhic* formalism."[6]

Stories are told by patients who find a balm in them, and a way of communicating with visitors and family. All patients and all families have a story. The stories that are generated by patients' experiences and the "stories" in which our ethical standards are embedded have become an increasingly important part of ethical discussions in philosophical and academic circles.[7] But stories are eccentric, and it has been difficult to draw principles from their aggregate. Each of us dies in a different way, as Sherwin Nuland says in his recent book *How We Die*.[8] Because that is so vital a truth, we must find a way to balance absolutes like the notion that "each moment of life is of infinite value," with the reality in which people experience death: cost, despair, inevitable loss in spite of end-stage delay of dying, treatment by physicians, and the extent of each personal experience with pain. Jews will continue to debate whether that should be so, but it *will* be so, of that there is no doubt.[9]

A PERSONAL LOOK AT NARRATIVE

I do not write as a medical ethicist, but as a student of narrative, and as a rabbi who has had significant experience as a hospital patient. I have served as chaplain, and participate on boards and committees designing training programs for spiritual counselors. I teach students about visiting in hospitals. My parents have died, my mother after an extended dooming illness accompanied by a thousand ethical decisions. My father's death, more recent, required no ethical thought, but rather an adjustment to the abrupt demise caused by the angel's kiss. The contrast is not irrelevant to my own way of looking at this problem - to my own story, in other words. In my hospital work I concentrate on the lived experience of the patient, and the ways in which people might help patients live through their experiences towards a more positive outcome. This "positive outcome" applies whether or not death occurs. I have been concerned with helping professionals develop more spiriting attitudes towards patients rather than with specific decisions in particular concrete situations.[10] My training in literature and personal experience have helped me concentrate on developing a kind of helping person, and have led me to be less interested in deciding this or that action in this or that case. But I have had to help people die. There are times when my commitment to the general welfare of people and to their morale has had to give way to recommendations in particular circumstances. Stories have helped me in that task, though less naturally than they help in thinking about ideals or the kinds of people that society can produce. One of the ways to use stories for reflecting on death and dying lies in some of the thinking about what literature is all about.

A MASTER STORY

I have called my discussion "Rabbi Judah's Handmaid", because of a story in the Talmud which records the death of this Mishnaic sage. Rabbi Judah was so important that he is often known only as "Rabbi". (The story is called a *ma'aseh* in Hebrew.) When the *ma'aseh* begins, the reader knows that "Rabbi" is dead; and that his death was a matter of great distress to his disciples. The unit as a whole comes at the end of a long discussion about death and property rights, great leaders, and public attitudes about death and memory.[11]

Tractate *Ketubot* 104a (Soncino translation) -

On the day when Rabbi (Judah) died, the rabbis decreed a public fast and offered prayers for heavenly mercy. They, furthermore, announced that whoever said that Rabbi was dead would be stabbed with a sword.

Rabbi's handmaid ascended the roof and prayed: "The immortals desire Rabbi to join them and the mortals desire Rabbi to remain with them; may it be the will of God that the mortals may overpower the immortals." When, however, she saw how often he resorted to the privy, painfully taking off his tefillin and putting them on again, she prayed: "May it be the will of God that

65

the immortals may overpower the mortals." As the Rabbis continued their prayers for heavenly mercy, she took up a jar and threw it down from the roof to the ground. At that moment they ceased praying and the soul of Rabbi departed to its eternal rest.

AN INITIAL EXPLICATION OF THIS STORY

This fairly well-known passage looks at first blush like an innocent *aggadah*, a specific kind of rabbinic tale, whose conclusion has application to questions about the termination of life. It is what Gerald Prince calls a "minimal story" - one which moves from a simple predictable state to a major shift in expected conclusion based on one thing that happens within the story.[12] Many contemporary thinkers have assigned the passage as a foundational source, a *locus classicus*, for the principle that while death may not be hastened according to Jewish law, it is permissible to halt an artificial intervention, if the patient would expire soon and naturally if we left him/her alone. The principle of getting in the way of obstacles to death, in this case the prayers of the rabbis is enunciated in the *Shulhan Arukh, Yoreh Deah,* specifically in the gloss of Moses Isserles.[13]

The relevant passage in the *Shulhan Arukh* does not cite the *Ketubot* passage, but it *does* use the same principle when it draws on the 12th Century work *Sefer Hasidim.*[14] There it is noted that if the sound of chopping wood is inhibiting the onset of inevitable death, we may stop the woodchoppers' chopping.

CONVENTIONAL HALAKHIC PRINCIPLES AND THE STORY

Thus the phrase *mesir hamoneia,* removing the impediment, is a term which has formal *halakhic* status within Jewish discourse. The phrase could also be utilized to consider the difference between letting death take its natural course, and stimulating the death process. If we stimulate the death process, we would be crossing the boundary into actively taking a life. The preservation of this boundary is important to anyone who would limit human encroachment on the divine, or for that matter, anyone who would establish human limits for any spiritual purpose. Among the severe exponents of a strict boundary is Rabbi J. David Bleich who notes:

> Any positive act designed to hasten the death of the patient is equated with murder in Jewish law, even if the death is hastened only by a matter of moments. ...Only the Creator, who bestows the gift of life, may relieve man of that life, even when it has become a burden rather than a blessing.[15]

For Bleich, we must keep the respirator going.

Some ethicists have managed to retain the principle of "the infinite value of life" while finding ways to move from respiration to brain waves as the index for life. Rosner appears to argue that they are one and the same. When we do adopt brain wave as the criterion, death will occur sooner in almost every case, since there is no way to extend brain wave activity in the way we extend respiratory activity. Others have suggested redefinition of the *goses*, and rely on redefining that term to achieve moderation. In high technological times, the three day period for *goses* no longer makes sense, in other words. I have already mentioned the excellent work of such people as Dorff and Gordis who seem to invoke classical norms while arriving at more relevant contemporary conclusions. In one form or another, such thinkers understand the law as containing the flexibility to combine the ideal principle with existential reality.

CASTING OFF A VENERATED PRINCIPLE

Among scientists the embrace of a less strict distinction between life and death appears just on the horizon. This appears to be true even among scientists committed to exploring humanistic implications. So, Sherwin Nuland argues against extending life at all costs:

> "At any given moment, some five percent of our nation's elderly reside in long-term care facilities... What do all of these old people die of? Though their doctors dutifully record such distinct entities as stroke, or cardiac failure, or pneumonia, these aged folk have in fact died because something in them has worn out."[16]

Nuland's statement reflects some of the sociological considerations which I have cited earlier. He leads his readers towards the view that a few more days of life is not what is consequential; and towards accepting the idea that life quality is relevant in bio-ethical discourse. As this general attitude becomes more widespread, it will subvert any Jewish norm that argues the infinite value of every moment of life. We shall slowly find ourselves thinking differently about the importance of extending life. The term *mesir hamoneia,* aborting the impediment to a natural death process, as cited in *Yoreh Deah* will slowly change its implications. The time will come when we no longer give antibiotics for the pneumonia of an elderly cardiac patient. The time has already come when we may not give the newest experimental drug to all patients with the same disease. The need to perform surgical procedures on elderly people will become less clear-cut. And the community surrounding the ill person will be more distant from that illness than ever before, and less inclined to counter-act economic reality with personal passion. Nuland's book takes us toward a rejection of Bleich's view of the human condition; and by extension, towards modulating the way in which we view tradition. But Nuland, despite his creativity, is only a formal expression of what is already being thought

68

implicitly. That modulation would sound something like this: Only the creator can take away the life which "He" has given, and only the Creator can continue to create the same life. Medicine confronts us with the possibility both of taking away life and creating it, and while either activity should belong only to God, we as agents in either case must view ourselves as partners with God in either case.[17]

Current methods of ethical inquiry may become out of date unless we incorporate unmediated human experience into the discussion of our principles. We must do so without cluttering the discussion with a thousand eccentric narratives.

TRADITIONAL TEXT IN CONTEMPORARY DISCOURSE

Even in the midst of this weighty discussion about life and death, I remain concerned about the place of traditional literature in the lives of Jews. The rift between *halakhic* thinking and what happens in actual situations will eventually lead to a cavalier attitude toward the very tradition that could contribute so richly to the discourse. In some way, the preservation of Jewish sources, and the active use of them, has more to do with developing a Jewish future than with solving any particular ethical dilemma. From my perspective, our traditionless world needs Judaism; but its modes will not be fully useful unless there is some richer meeting with narrative eccentricity.

To encourage rapprochement I will examine some principles of narrative, especially as they emerge from the story of Rabbi Judah. Let me begin my approach to narrative thinking through a statement about aspects of language and its functions. The statement is mine, and I acknowledge at the outset that the subject is more complex than is reflected here.

FUNCTIONS OF LANGUAGE

Language, through speech or writing, has at least four functions for our purposes here:

1. It can reflect reality, and it can attempt to come close to depicting a thing through its use of figures of speech, measurement, and analogy, as it is shaped into sentences and paragraphs.

2. It can give a construction to reality - a kind of hermeneutic representation in which the listener and the speaker derive a sense of meaning from what is said, and from the way it is said.

3. It can dramatize a situation to convince a reader of a certain attitude, or to encourage action. It may be used to enhance sympathy or antipathy for the situation being described. Language, in other words, has a strong rhetorical function.[18]

4. It can constitute the reality. In other words, there are certain contracts, ontological states, that are brought into being by the utterance which creates the reality. An example might be the very "pronouncement" by a physician that "the patient is dead"; but, of course, the most common sense of this term is the naming of things, clerical performance of marriage rites, and the Creator's bringing into being with "a word". The more sophisticated idea that narrative is itself an imitation of speech acts is not relevant to the shape I am giving this discussion; but it is dutifully noted here.

Most ethical decision making draws heavily on the first kind of speech. Here is a rule or a principle, and over there is a circumstance. Is the circumstance over there like the circumstance which the original rule maker had in mind? Is a respirator, in other words, like the woodchoppers' chopping or the Rabbis' praying? I this instance, a "story" might be used to modify or clarify or disagree with the general rule which is being proposed.

But a fuller use of story or narrative as an independent form of speech represents the second function of speech: The giving of construction to reality. From that construction new meanings develop, and sometimes multiple meanings emerge. In this sense of speech, a partnership is always implicit between author, auditor or reader. And once these separate parties become partners, one must expect multiple interpretations. This is due to the nature of language which is always multivalent, and the nature of the reception, the way in which people hear or read. The language of the story and the particular situation of the auditor create different constructions of the same story and a different reality. If we grant this multiplicity of meaning, we must distinguish between the idea that a passage has *no* particular meaning and the notion that the passage may have various meanings for different auditors, or for the same auditor at different times.[19]

THE STORY REVISITED

Let us examine the story again:

> On the day that Rabbi Judah died, the Rabbis decreed a public fast and offered prayers for heavenly mercy. They, furthermore, announced that whoever said that Rabbi was dead would be stabbed with a sword.
>
> Rabbi's handmaid ascended the roof and prayed: "The immortals desire Rabbi to join them and the mortals desire Rabbi to remain with them; may it be the will of God that the mortals may overpower the immortals. When however, she saw how often he resorted to the privy, painfully taking off his tefillin and putting them on again, she prayed: "May it be the will of God that the

immortals may overpower the mortals." As the Rabbis continued their prayers for heavenly mercy, she took up a jar and threw it down from the roof to the ground. At that moment they ceased praying and the soul of Rabbi departed to its eternal rest.

Our second reading is an opportunity to focus on elements within the *ma'aseh* that carry a reader beyond the straightforward plot of the "minimal story", to other dimensions and themes, to its rhetorical strength and possibilities for surprise.

My discussion of this second reading will take place by way of three perspectives on narrative: One from a psychologist-philosopher, Jerome Bruner; one from a literary theorist, J. Hillis Miller; and one from a legal scholar, the late Robert Cover. These three inventive thinkers by no means exhaust the theoretical issues which might be available to this discussion of narrative. In addition the world's great story tellers stand in the background of this discussion in the telling and retelling an infinity of new tales based on the finite number of received themes and narrative patterns.

ONE CONVENTIONAL USE OF NARRATIVE

One may begin the discussion of narrative ethics with two sets of polarities. The first marks the difference between the particular facts of the sickroom with its messy reality and sometimes fuzzy areas of management, on the one hand, and the clean and terse conclusions of principles as enunciated in the *Shulhan Arukh*, on the other. Responsa that draw on the *Shulhan Arukh* sometimes embellish the decision of a rabbi, *poseq*, with stories of exceptional circumstances, application of one set of circumstances to another, etc., but always express some level of abstraction in their conclusion. They inevitably revert to the guiding principles behind an issue. This kind of story telling preserves the principle enunciated in the code, as I think can be said of Kantian ethical discussions.

The other polarity has to do with the nature of rabbinic narrative upon which principles are based. On the normative pole in this set of polarities, one must not forget that within the rabbinic frame of mind, the stories recorded in the Talmudic material represent actual events which happened within a condition of divine providence. Thus in the rabbinic view, the results represent a sense of the way the world ought to be.[20] On the other pole, is the modern secular view of story, which argues that stories are not meant to be apodictic guides to behavior, but rather have much to do with developing the imagination and the perceptual capabilities of readers or listeners. For people who think this way, an overly utilitarian view of literature's function stifles imagination and brings death to the perceptual world. In secular literary theory there is no death more serious than death to the perceptual world.[21] Both of these attitudes may be at work to some degree and often at the same time. Stories sometimes guide us to specific conclusions, but at other times they exist primarily to enrich our imagination. Narrative reality is more easily related to the second of these purposes.

INDUCTIVE USE OF THE STORY

Let me now examine the elements in the handmaid's story that tell us something about narrative reality. These elements of narrative reality will help us decide what to do in the case of a patient who is likely to die in the very near future; but they can only *help* us decide. I will then proceed to extract certain principles of narrative which explain or describe these points.

In the first place, the Talmudic story seems to rely on the assumption that the reader would pray for the extended life of Rabbi Judah. The story is important because the conclusion is different from that expectation. Connected to that surprising outcome is the mitigating circumstance which accounts for the change in expectation: the extreme pain of Rabbi.[22] We must also notice that the story may deal with other issues as the power of human prayer, the importance of a woman, or the non-importance of women in that society. Finally, it draws on the idea that witnessing an instance of suffering may lead to a change of mind.[23] Within this little story itself the maid's experience of Rabbi Judah is not simply reported, but described as having occurred many times. The frequent visits to the privy, and the repeated action of removing his *tefilin* and putting them on again, are indices - metonymies of his pain.

Each of these elements attaches to an essential aspect of narrative theory. These aspects of narrative take us beyond the more direct use of the *aggadah's* conclusion as our ethical guide.[24] I am *not* arguing that because this story "justifies" letting Rabbi Judah die we therefore have a comfortable precedent for letting people die.[25] The story is too complex to limit its meaning to the *halakhic* principle *mesir hamoneia*.

I *will* argue that there are principles in this story which may influence decisions about the care of an aging parent who is "just hanging on." Other principles in the story may illuminate the condition of those who stand by to help. The story could support extending the parent's life or ending it. The story may remind us that the ill parent will certainly die in the very near future, with the time spent barely breathing, filled with tubes, medicine and discomfort; or it may foster our extending life while friends rally as community to encourage the ill person. I do not propose that narrative theory stimulates specific emotions or spiritual impulses nor does it tap the emotions of otherwise cool thinking formalists. I seek narrative principles which can shed light on the way we *do* make decisions and the way we *ought to* make decisions.

THREE THEORIES

Narrative and Learning - Jerome Bruner

Distinguished senior Harvard philosopher, psychologist and cognitive theorist, Bruner approaches narrative out of his particular interest in epistemology. He advances the following argument: "Let me begin by setting out my argument as baldly as possible...There are two irreducible modes of cognitive functioning, ...Each provides ways of organizing representation in memory and of filtering the perceptual world. ...One seeks explications that are context free and universal, and the other seeks explications that are context sensitive and particular. ... one mode is centered around the narrow epistemological question of how to know the truth; and the other around the broader and more inclusive question of the meaning of experience. (Note above, the various functions of speech.) ...The imaginative application of the paradigmatic mode leads to good theory, tight analysis, logical proof, and empirical discovery guided by reasoned hypothesis". (Bruner here is more absolutist than he needs to be.) "...As noted, narrative is concerned with the explication of human intentions in the context of action." (He goes on to say that narratives do not occur in an entirely unrestricted fashion, but that...) "most narratives that create an aura of believable life-likeness involve a recounting of an initial canonical steady state, its breach, an ensuing crisis, and a redress, with limited accompanying states of awareness in the protagonists."

Bruner has also focussed on the length of time the narrative can reflect. He has called this "narrative diachronicity." [26] Professional literary theorists have dealt at greater length with the phenomenon, both its power and the techniques for achieving it.[27]

75

Narrative and Law - Robert Cover

Cover, the late Yale law professor, wrote about the place of interpretive pluralism and normative thinking within both the Jewish legal heritage and the American constitutional tradition. Cover emphasizes that acts which signify something new gain their significance if we understand them in reference to a norm.[28] Cover's "Nomos", meaning law, norm or principle, takes place within a narrative which then often generates its own nomos:

> A legal tradition is part and parcel of a complex normative world. The tradition includes not only a *corpus juris*, but also a language and a mythos-narratives in which the *corpus juris* is located by those whose wills act upon it. These myths establish the paradigms for behavior. They build relations between the normative and the material universe, between the constraints of reality and the demands of an ethic.

> Law may be viewed as a system of tension or a bridge linking a concept of a reality to an imagined alternative - that is, as a connective between two states of affairs, both of which can be represented in their normative significance only through the devices of narrative. Thus one constitutive element of a *nomos* is the phenomenon George Steiner has labeled "alternity", the other than the case, the counterfactual propositions, images, shapes of will and evasion with which we charge our mental being and by means of which we build the changing, largely fictive milieu for our somatic and our social existence.[29] ...Our visions hold our reality up to us as unredeemed.

I understand Cover to mean that the normative pattern may recommend a way the world would look if it were redeemed, and the narrative may represent the world as it is lived. This does not mean that the narrative world determines our choices over the norms; Cover insists that the narrative cannot take place without the normative being folded in to it. Efforts to split narrative and norms into two distinct categories of argument are not legitimate for understanding how either of them works. Cover's contribution, for my purposes, is to remind us to keep playing the norm, or fixed value, against the dynamism of the narrative reality. That is what produces true *juris-generativity*, the ability of the law to grow.

Narrative and Ethics - J. Hillis Miller

Miller calls our attention on the act of reading. The most radical elements in his thought have a congruence with certain Kabbalistic modes of thought.[30] Miller has expressed his position in a variety of formats, so I will paraphrase and quote directly:

"The Moral law gives rise by an intrinsic necessity to storytelling, even if that storytelling in one way or another puts in question or subverts the moral law. Ethics and narration cannot be kept separate, though their relation is neither symmetrical nor harmonious." For Miller, the primary ethical act in reading is choosing text's meaning, and thus "renouncing" the reading one rejects. Reading is multivalent because of the nature of language. He suggests that this renunciation is allegorized in narratives where characters make the same choices within the plots as readers. For Miller, then, reading involves a non-medical "triage", based on the finite authority of language and its inability to wrap perfectly around an idea. Language has the same limited resources for its task as the community for keeping people healthy. Whether our language reflects reality, interprets reality or brings things into being, our results are imperfect. Choices have to be made and in both reading and life. A non-medical triage is an operative principle. Here is an affinity with Luria's notion of *tzimtzum*, which is the source of all limits; and it is enforced in the final chapter of Miller's *Ethics of Reading*, where he draws on Henry James' image of a white field against which writing (and presumably reading as a consequence of writing) resembles dark footsteps in the snow. We can only walk one way at a time. We may decide to let our aging sick patient live longer, or we may decide the opposite. Either decision involves a renunciation of the alternative. We may find that our family story strengthens any resolve; or it may cause us to preserve the Jewish norm of the infinite value of life. A family story may even require preserving the warmth we feel in the presence of a loved person, no matter how much pain that person is suffering. When we read a story of illness, as in the case of R. Judah, we are committing the act which Miller identifies as *prosopopeia*: the imaginative creation of a reality out of nothing more than black letters on a white page. This ability to create will be a vital part of our decision making at the bedside of a loved on who is probably going to die.

Miller's stance, is radically free of the emphasis on "moral ending", and reminds us how far we are from thinking deeply about narrative. Most readers seem to use stories for ethics as an opportunity to try alternatives of action. Most critics accept this as one legitimate use of story. But Miller's more complex allegorical sense of reading is a direction which has great significance when applied to the decisions which face us in life and death situations. These situations require a triage which underpins all stories in the hospital and which force health care givers to deal with the idealization of life and its infinite value. For while the principle of the infinite value of life is an important spiritual baseline for the ethicist, the stories of people's lives always reveal compromises. The story of society's continuity compromises us even further. Society cannot continue to provide infinite amounts of medical care.[31] These three narrative theorists, selected from many other, provide us with guidelines about the nature of story and its relationship to ethical behavior.

78

There must be one additional literary pause in our thinking. The history of story telling and story writing is a history of re-writing, of recasting old themes or original simple tales, into more complex novels, dramas and epics. Basic story outlines are always retold. Sometimes they reach the same conclusion, but include more characters or subplots; and on other occasions the additional material leads to a different story with new conclusions. I suggest that the story of Rabbi Judah can be used in a similar way in our contemporary and more complicated "stories".[32]

A LAST LOOK AT THE STORY

Let us return for a final time to the story of Rabbi Judah and his handmaid. What is this story about? It may be about the power of love to change one's mind or simply about the changing of mind. It may reveals that real emotions come from particularities and details, she saw how he suffered and how often he went to the privy. It may be about the power of human prayer, and thus support Cover's and Suzanne Stone's position about the partnership between humans and the divine, not to mention Jewish thinkers like Greenberg and Borowitz.[33] It may be a tale of mitigating circumstances: we *ought to* take this action, but we *are forced to take* the second action. The story of Rabbi Judah's death should, then, not be the *locus classicus* for a particular action or decision, but a model for the uses of narrative. Like all good stories, it makes explicit the actual experience of the lived life. The lived life which sometimes competing with norms dominates the ethical decisions we make and the compromises which are an inevitable part of them. The preservation of the principle may not be threatened so much by reality as enhanced by it. Yet if reality shell enhance principle instead of struggle with it, we must find a way to connect between life's uncertainty and the clarity of principle in narrative. An inventory may help us:

1) The Rabbi Judah story captures a sense of the duration of his illness, which mirrors very much what happens in the hospital room of dying people. The principle of preserving life often makes a moral sense at the beginning of a long period of suffering, or when discussed in the abstract, and less after sixty days or ninety days, and repeated experience of pain.[34] While my mother's slope to her death from a malignant brain tumor led me, my sisters and father from urging aggressive treatment to the more modulated impulse to let go, the very length of her illness had an important positive effect on relationships within our family. How much would have been lost between us in the building of our family story, which included her heroism and our relationships with each other, had she died significantly sooner? In other words, we carried a story into the episode which influenced our thinking; and we remain with a rewritten story when the experience is over. (Bruner's sense of time, grounded in Ricoeur.)

2) The R. Judah story demonstrates from within itself the varying possibilities of the story. The question of the meaning of life and of the lives of the survivors is allegorized within the story. (Miller's notion of allegory.)

3) Creating a reality through the reading of the story is a necessary part of the creativity which themodern reader must employ in reaching decisions. (Miller above.)

4) The story has multiple meanings, which rely on the context of the reader and the story and are congruent with the centrality of context in making ethical decisions in the lived hospital room. (Cover's citation of Steiner and other traditional narrative thinkers remind us of this.)

5) The story contains a mitigating circumstance in its context which represents the first step in the shift from the canonical expectation that we pray for our loved ones to live longer, until we get a real sense of their pain. (Bruner and Cover.)

6) The story affords the opportunity, for the reader to exchange himself/herself for various characters within the story. In a typical family, there may be siblings, a parent, a patient, and a doctor and friends committed to a specific kind of treatment, as well. (George Steiner on alternity.)

7) The story may be rewritten in a contemporary context which includes new economic realities; different ways of looking at priorities; and, for good or ill, increasing valorization of individual experience. (Wallace Martin.)

8) The act of narration may be an act of reflection on the event or events. The conclusion, then, may be less significant than the process.

9) The story includes a renunciation as Rabbi Judah's maid cannot have it both ways. She makes a choice; doctors make choices and the families of dying people make choices. (Miller)

How would this use of narrative work in a real case? It should not be used on the spot in the midst of any particular medical crisis. The use of narrative thinking is more ambient in nature. Families often need time before their members can agree on the meanings of the words being used, especially in cases of durable powers of attorney or living wills. I have encountered the phrase " not to take extraordinary measures" dozens of times, and almost no two interpretations are the same. Narrative thinking might help people reflect on these and other meanings, but probably not under the pressure of specific crises. Yet as an overarching way of approaching bio-ethical problems, a story has much value; and for those of us who must work professionally in these critical circumstances provides much guidance. It would give the agents and the subjects of a medical situation the knowledge that they are part of a long tradition of others who faced ethical dilemmas. Secondly, it may clarify the different contexts in which the principles of inquiry may take place. Third, it highlights the reality in which we make ethical compromise. It will, in addition, give a sense that the time may, after all, have come to let a loved one go. It may also be used to help vulnerable people understand the importance of the relationships with the others who surround them in these critical situations. Would I or my family have reached a better decision about my mother's life had we thought more formally or in a more explicitly narrative way? I cannot tell; but I am convinced that no system would have been perfectly adequate, and the doctor's opinion was never enough!

CONCLUSION

Among the most powerful people in our culture are doctors. As they study diseases and seek a cure, they have god-like moments. That is why medical training is so focussed on disease. Nuland calls this "the riddle" which must be solved, but which often gets in the way of treating the patient as a full human being. When the disease and its riddle get folded into the human being who carries an illness, the doctor becomes more human, more tragic, and more a partner with the person served. Her doctors fulfill a real partnership with the Creator. To "be human" is to take the risk that the absolute code is broken in the effort to serve the lived narrative world with its many shapes and too many meanings.

In a distinguished collection of essays, the philosopher Yeshayahu Leibowitz affirms "*halakhic* formalism" as a necessary mode of Jewish ethical decision making.[35] Yet, in an article in the same collection, he speaks about doctors' healing roles in a slightly different tone. There he cites Maimonides on medical treatment in a way which suggests reversing formalism: "Treatment of a patient is not directed towards an abstract concept, but rather towards the actual sick person. Every ill person is different from every other ill person - even though they may have the same illness. And, thus, the doctor must cure the sick person and not the disease." [36] It is, similarly, the patient who dies.

82

Jewish law is devoted partially to preserving a tradition and a community. Thus our management of death as a general subject is formal and communal. It strives towards a level and synchronic consensus, and it insists that no life is more important than any other life. It strives for one level in our thinking and our action. The management of individual deaths, however, is another matter; it is a many storied affair.

Notes

1. A *goses* has generally been defined as a person with 72 hours left to live. It is a measure that is coming under close scrutiny because of our ability to prolong life. Helpful sources for the concept are *Mishnah Arakhin* 1:3, and *Babylonian Talmud Kiddushin* 71b.

2. Elliot N. Dorff, "A Methodology for Jewish Medical Ethics," *Jewish Law Association Studies, VI,* B. S. Jackson and S. M. Passamaneck, eds., Atlanta, 1992.

3. This paper grows out of a workshop I conducted at the Jewish healing conference: *Refaeinu,* sponsored by the Jewish Healing Center and the Nathan Cummings Foundation in Winter, 1994. Special thanks to Rabbi Nancy Flam and her staff for giving me the opportunity to put forth the tentative ideas that emerged into this more fully developed work.

4. J. David Bleich, in many places, but especially, *Judaism and Healing,* Hoboken, 1981. My most vivid memory of Bleich's explication of this came at a medical ethics seminar at Cedars Sinai Medical Center. A frustrated physician fumed at Bleich's strictness, and tried to illustrate how foolish was his position, and began a thought with the statement: "Rabbi Bleich, I have a terminal patient on the 7th floor who..." Bleich interrupted him with the quip: "Dr. X, we are all terminal."

5. Several contemporary thinkers have moved closer to changing the ways we think about ethics. For a summary of the different efforts to deal with new technological and social realities, and to embrace, at least partially, modern ways of reading literary texts, refer to Elliot Dorff's article, (note 2). Jewish thinkers who are especially important in this regard have been:
David Ellenson, "How to Draw Guidance from a Heritage," in *A Time to be Born and a Time to Die,* Barry Kogan, ed., Boston, 1991.
Daniel Gordis, "Wanted - The Ethical in Jewish Bio-Ethics," *Judaism* 38/1 Winter, 1989.
Irving Greenberg, "Toward a Covenantal Ethic of Medicine," in *Jewish Values in Bioethics,* Levi Meier, ed., Boston, 1986.
Louis Newman, "Woodchoppers and Respirators: The Problem of Interpretation in Contemporary Jewish Ethics," *Modern Judaism* 10/1, February, 1990.

6. The term is coined by Daniel Gordis, and used by David Ellenson. Their work is noted above. Formalist ethical thinking, or at least citation of specific sources, characterizes even the most radically dissenting Jewish position on active euthanasia. See Byron L. Sherwin, "Euthanasia: A Jewish View", *The Journal of Aging and Judaism*, Fall, 1987. A more personal statement is contained in Daniel Jeremy Silver, "The Right to Die?" in *Jewish Reflections on Death*, Jack Riemer, ed., New York, 1974.

7. Here I want to mention two especially important works for the development of my own thinking-- one from general ethical discourse, and one from the religious domain:

Martha C. Nussbaum, *Love's Knowledge*, Essays on Philosophy and Literature, Oxford, 1990.

Stanley Haurwas, *Truthfulness and Tragedy*, South Bend, 1977. (My thanks to Rabbi Alan Henkin for introducing me to this work and for his wonderful explications).

8. Sherwin Nuland, *How We Die*, New York, 1994. See especially Nuland's final chapter, "The Lessons Learned."

9. Here I am speaking of more than harmonizing through the case method that Dorff so eloquently; and I am attempting to move beyond the creativity suggested by David Hartman, Irving Greenberg, (noted above,) and even Louis Newman and Daniel Gordis.

10. See Martha Nussbaum, above, for a description of her notion that the kind of life we lead may be more important than any specific action we take.

11. For a rich understanding of the nature of the *sugya* I am indebted to Prof. David Kraemer of the Jewish Theological Seminary - to his work and his personal comments; and I am grateful, as always when I venture into these waters, to my colleagues David Ellenson, Elliot Dorff, and Rachel Adler. Professor Ronald Garet of the University of Southern California has encouraged my exploration of narrative theory and law.

12. See Gerald Prince, *A Grammar of Stories*, Boston, 1973; cited in Wallace Martin, *Recent Theories of Narrative*, Ithica, 1986, p. 95.

13. The passage is cited in several articles on Jewish bio-ethics and the termination of life: Louis Newman, Elliot Dorff, as above. For a more canonical discussion, see Fred Rosner, "Rabbi Moshe Feinstein on the Treatment of the Terminally Ill", *Judaism*, 37:2, 1988. See *Babylonian Talmud, Avodah Zara*, 18a, and Rosner's qualifications based on *Horayot* 13a regarding the infinite value of life. Solomon Freehof utilizes the story in one instance in a discussion on alleviation of pain. *American Reform Responsa*, Walter Jacob, ed., New York, 1983, #76, pp. 253ff.

14. *Shulhan Arukh, Yoreh Deah* 339:2. The note from Isserles, *(ReMa)* is translated in most English editions.

15. J. David Bleich, *Judaism and Healing*, Hoboken, 1981, p. 135

16. *Op. Cit.* p. 44

17. The so-called "covenantal" ethicisits have already begun to talk this way. See especially Ellenson and Greenberg, above.

18. For more on this subject, one should read: I. A. Richards, "Four Kinds of Meaning," *Practical Criticism*, New York, 1929; also available in *Critical Theory Sicne Plato*, Hazard Adams ed., New York, 1971; and Paul Ricoeur, *Time and Narrative*, vol. 2, trans. McLaughlin and Pellauer, Chicago, 1984.

19. In this regard, see Suzanne Last Stone, "In Pursuit of the Counter-Text: The Turn to the Jewish Legal Model in Contemporary American Legal Theory," *Harvard Law Review*, vol. 106, #4, February, 1993.

For a discussion of the educational relevance of joining post-modern linguistic concerns with reception theory, see William Cutter, "Owning Meaning in a Pluralistic Age," *Religious Education*, Winter, 1987.

20. On this matter, see David Stern, *Parables in Midrash, Narrative and Exegesis in Rabbinic Literature*, Boston, 1991. This position is not without some controversy, as can be seen in disagreements between Jonah Fraenkel and Dan Ben Amos. A helpful discussion of some of these problems is available in the unpublished M. A. Thesis of Rabbi Andrea Weiss, "Tell Them, and Tell Them Again: A Literary Analysis of Parallel Midrashic and Talmudic Sage Stories," Hebrew Union College - Jewish Institute of Religion, 1993. The reader may wish to see Dan Ben-Amos, "Generic Distinctions in the Aggadah," in *Studies in Jewish Folklore*, Frank Talmage ed., New York, 1980.

21. Murray Krieger, "An Apology for Poetics," contained in *Critical Theory Since* 1965, Adams and Searle eds., Gainesville, 1986, originally contained in *American Criticism in the Poststructuralist Age*, Ira Konigsberg ed., Ann Arbor, 1981. This struggle is as old as literary criticism, and is dramatically demonstrated in the work of critics as different as Wayne Booth of University of Chicago, and Walter Benjamin, the legendary German thinker and essayist of the 1920's and 30's.

22. Those who know Talmud will recognize Rabbi Judah's legendary digestive illness from other passages. *Baba Metzia* 85a.

23. The prayer notion would fit into the paradigm set forth by Suzanne Stone both because it contains multiple meanings and because one of those meanings has to do with the power of people to effect the supernal world. See Freehof.

24. On this one may see controversy aplenty as between writers like Giles Gunn, Robert Coles, A. Bartlett Giamati, J. Hillis Miller, Wayne Booth, Martha Nussbaum, Nel Noddings, and a host of other thinkers who have wrestled with the place of story in the derivation of ethical principles or the specific conclusions in specific problematic circumstances. In various ways, anyone who has written on this subject has to face the more restricted sense of "the moral" in the story to which most casual readers revert, which is promoted by such writers as John Gardner, in his *On Moral Fiction*, New York, 1977.

25. This material was originally presented at the conference, *Refa'enu*, sponsored by the Jewish Healing Center and The Nathan Cummings Foundation. Many of my listeners at these workshops were concerned that I was creating a Jewish version of the soft, caring and broadly moral outlook embedded in some radical feminist thinking and in even some of the tough minded thinking of people like Nel Noddings and Carol Gilligan. Justice Harry Blackmun had been criticized for overly generalized thinking from time to time. Jeffrey Rosen, *New Republic* commentator, has been critical of the Justice in this regard. See the April 29th issue of the magazine and Carol Gilligan, *In a Different Voice*, Boston, 1982, and subsequent research reports as well as Nel Noddings, *Caring, A Feminine Approach to Ethics and Moral Education*, Berkley, 1984.

26. See Jerome Bruner, "The Narrative Construction of Reality," *Critical Inquiry*, 18/1, Autumn, 1991. The most comprehensive treatment of time in narrative is found in Paul Ricoeur, *Time and Narrative*, (original in French in 3 volumes). On the "technique" used in the Rabbi Judah story, see vol. 2, p. 71.

27. Wallace Martin, *Op. Cit.* p. 168 contains a lucid overview of the issue of time, summarizing some of Ricoeur's thought along with that of others.

28. Robert Cover, "Nomos and Narrative." in *Harvard Law Review*, vol. 97/4, 1982 See also "Obligation: A Jewish Jurisprudence of the Social Order," *Journal of Law and Religion*, Vol. 5, pp. 65-74.

29. See George Steiner, *After Babel*, Oxford, 1981, p. 222. I am grateful to Prof. Ron Garet of the University of Southern California for suggestions and guidance about the work of Cover.

30. See especially, Miller, *The Ethics of Reading*, New York, 1987, and *Versions of Pygmalion*, Boston, 1990. Critics have included Frederic Crews I am thinking especially of the last chapter of Miller's *Ethics of Reading* and its treatment of Henry James discussion of *The Golden Bowl*. See William Cutter, "Renouncing Simplicity," *Religious Education*, Summer, 1993 for an effort to domesticate Miller within a Jewish and religious ethical context.

31. I use the word "triage" somewhat informally. The term appears to come from a First World War practice whereby French medics had to divide groups of wounded into one of three categories for purposes of deciding who gets help. I use it, loosely as I suggest, to mean the inevitable exercise of selection wherever infinite wish collides with finite reality.

WILLIAM CUTTER

32. See Wallace Martin, *Op. Cit.* p. 170 for a discussion of these feature of narrative.

33. See also David Hartman, "Moral Uncertainties in the Practice of Medicine: The Dynamics of Interdependency from a Halakhic Perspective," *The Journal of Medicine and Philosophy*, 1979, vol. 4, #1.

34. See Ernst Cassel, *The Nature of Suffering and the Goals of Medicine*, Oxford, 1991, especially chapter 1.

35. Yeshayahu Leibowitz, "The General and the Particular in the Theory of Medical Practice," (Hebrew) and "Medical Practice and Values," (Hebrew) in *Emunah, Historiah veArakhim*, Tel Aviv, 1982. Leibowitz makes a bold distinction between the principle that one cannot "permit" a life to be terminated, and the possibility that doctors may make certain decisions to terminate without asking for a Jewish judgment about the application of the principle.

36. Y. Leibowitz, *Op. Cit.* pp. 240-241.

END-STAGE EUTHANASIA
Some Other Considerations

Walter Jacob

Death and euthanasia bring us face to face with some of the basic problems of modern medical ethics. The advances in medical technology have caused problems for the patient and family, the health care institution and its personnel, as well as the government. The matter, however, goes far beyond medical technology and its advances.

Judaism has always been a highly optimistic religion with a love of life which permeates every aspect of it. That positive view has come from the creation story with its continuous refrain "and it was good." For human life, the statement went even further, "and it was very good." Life had supreme value and was to be sustained even through the violation of other Divine commandments. This thought was paramount and all commandments except those which forbade murder, incest, and idolatry could be voided to save a human life.[1] This has meant that any thought of killing another person even for some supposed benefit to that person was abhorrent.[2]

Euthanasia has, therefore, been completely foreign to Judaism. The stance of Judaism was absolutely clear in the interpretion of the early rabbinic literature, the later codes and the subsequent responsa. We continue to take this as our normative position. We reject efforts to eliminate individuals with genetic defects. The only possible exception to this rule may be end-stage euthanasia which we wish to discuss in this essay.

A variety of issues demand our attention. A new light has been shed on the traditional way of looking at euthanasia by my colleagues Peter Knobel and Leonard Kravitz in their papers. As I have also shown elsewhere, the Orthodox hesitation about end-stage euthanasia has been established on a weak and largely anecdotal foundation. Furthermore two of the tales normally used actually point in a different direction.

The story of the execution of Haninah ben Teradion indicated that an outside party could assist someone to an easier death[3] while the story of the old woman who ceased her prayers and died after three days indicated that it is permissible for the individual involved to hasten his/her death as well.[4] These tales alone are enough to have us rethink our position toward end-stage euthanasia. We must take a variety of matters into consideration as we review end-stage euthanasia.

Let us begin with the role of healing and the physician in our Tradition. This has evolved and changed since Biblical times and again been altered in our own age. This has led to a different role for the physician in the decisions made at the end of life. We must review our understanding of quality of life concerns and our definition of the *goses*.

Finally, we must consider the economic consequences of medical procedures. These will ultimately determine governmental policy. In the expanding American economy of the latter part of the twentieth century, economic considerations have not played a major role. Medical technology has been allowed to progress with very few restrictions. We are, however, coming to the end of that period and realize that we are among the few countries in which we can discuss these issues before economic considerations overwhelm us. How shall we balance the limited funds available for medical use with extremely expensive technologies which may add only marginally to a human life? Our Tradition, along with other religious traditions, must address this issue otherwise it will be left entirely to the utilitarian forces of government.

Each of these matters will be discussed briefly with a full realization that we can only begin, perhaps to ask appropriate questions and point to some possible solutions.

HEALING AND THE JEWISH PHYSICIAN

We shall start with the status of healing and the physician within Judaism. They have certainly not been clearly delineated by the religion of Israel in Biblical times. A wide variety of passages indicate that God is the ultimate healer and also the source of disease, "If you will diligently harken to the voice of the Lord your God and will do that which is right in His eyes and will give ear to His commandments, keep all his statues, I will put none of the diseases upon you which I have put upon the Egyptians for I am the Lord who heals you," or a passage from the time of the kings: "In the thirty-ninth year of his reign Asa was diseased in his feet; his disease was exceedingly grave; yet in his disease he sought not the Lord, but the physicians, and Asa left with his fathers and died in the forty-first year of his reign." Jeremiah expresses some doubts: "Is there no balm in Gilead? Is there no physician there? Why then is not the health of the daughter of my people recovered?" Job is not enthusiastic: "Physicians are of no value."[5] These passages may represent two possible theological views. In the first, God controls and human beings have no autonomy. In the second, human beings possess autonomy, but, as Jews, have surrendered much of it through entering a covenant with God.

The Bible has also expressed two different views about healing; Exodus states: "And if men fight and one smite the other with a stone or with his fist and he does not die but stays in his bed, if he rises again and walks abroad upon his staff, then shall he that struck him be quit; only he shall pay for the loss of his time and shall cause him to be thoroughly healed."[6] A physician may have been involved in the healing process here.

In another place we hear of the foreign general Naaman who came to Israel seeking a cure, and he was healed by God. This dual view of God as the healer versus the physician was continued by the post-Biblical books which were excluded from the canon. Ben Sirach seems to feel that the physician's help should be sought, but he has been instructed by God while in the *Book of Tobit*, the physician did not succeed and Tobit was miraculously healed.[7]   The Bible was not particularly concerned with medicine in contrast to the other ancient Near Eastern societies as Egypt and Mesopotamia.[8]

Although no clear path was set by Scripture, the Mishnah, Talmud and Midrashim heavily favored medical intervention with numerous statements in praise of physicians as well as a few which cast doubt on their efforts.   This was part of the Hellenistic influence upon Judaism. Many texts take it for granted that physicians will be used, others require it, while a few would have those who are ill rely on God alone. The strongest negative feelings were expressed by the statement: "The best of physicians is destined for *gehenna,*" but even this statement assumed that physicians were widely used. Other texts make it clear that those who rely on the physician should not see this as a denial of God as the ultimate healer.[9]

In later Jewish times only Karaite writers continued to oppose medical intervention, however I do not know whether this was followed by the Karaite community which usually lived in close contact with rabbinate Jews. The medieval scholar/physicians do not comment on this behavior within the Karaite communities with which they must have been familiar.[10]

A few great medieval rabbinic scholars opposed or limited the use of medicine. Among them were Nahmanides who was himself a physician and Ibn Ezra who felt that a physician should appropriately deal only with external diseases.[11]

God remains as the ultimate healer for all rabbinic Jews as indicated by the liturgical paragraph in the *Amidah* which praises God "who heals the sick," a statement found in traditional and liberal prayer books.

In the Mishnaic period or a bit earlier, medical care by physicians became general.[12]   The discussion of anatomical details, numerous symptoms, and medical treatments in the Talmud and the later *halakhic* literature indicated that medical treatment and the intervention of the physician was normative. There are thousands of references scattered throughout the Talmudic and Midrashic literature, not to speak of the later responsa.[13] The detailed discussions encouraged all Jews to make a maximum use of whatever medical techniques existed.

These discussions, of course, continued in the later *halakhic* literature up to the present day. Despite the large number of references, no tractate of the Talmud dealt exclusively with medicine or medical ethics. The earliest Jewish medical treatise is the *Sefer Refuot* by Asaph. This major work may date from the eighth century.[14] Later, of course, there was a great deal of medical literature and a whole series of volumes by Maimonides along with references in his *Mishneh Torah*.[15]

Although there were few basic changes in medical practice from the Greco-Roman period until the eighteenth century, the older medicine had to be rediscovered in the Islamic period. When medical practices changed, Judaism accepted the new ways with little or no discussion.[16]

Why were changes in medical practice so readily accepted by the Jewish public? Theologically, although God was the ultimate healer, we felt that the covenant permitted us the freedom to seek medical treatment and even mandated it. The high status of the Jewish physicians was not due only to their skill, which was appreciated by the Gentile world as well, but because in many instances they combined rabbinic scholarship with medical knowledge. Maimonides is only the most illustrious example and the line of his predecessors can be traced to Theodos, Mar Samuel, R. Hiyyah and others of the second century. This unique combination of Jewish scholarship and medical knowledge provided authority to the physician. It placed the physician in a position of trust as well as religious leadership.

We can see this combination of gifts most clearly in Maimonides who described his tasks as a physician to Ibn Tibbon, his translator, in a famous letter.[17] The authority of the rabbinate was easily extended to the medical realm, and, in the case of Maimonides, to the realm of philosophy, an area about which many of his contemporaries had serious reservations.[18] The status of the physician and the willingness to follow the most recent medical technology was therefore more or less guaranteed from Talmudic times onward.

A residue of that trust remains to the present day, but it has diminished for two reasons: The general questioning of all authority and the shift of emphasis of the Jewish physician away from Jewish scholarship to medical knowledge alone. This is visible not only in matters of death and euthanasia but in other medical areas also.

Modern medical practitioners are usually specialists in a narrow field, and only rarely concern themselves with broader ethical questions. Furthermore, they often have only a vague interest in such questions. As the role of physicians has changed, their influence in "end of life" issues has diminished.

THE *GOSES*

Individuals who are dying have been placed into a special category by the Tradition called *goses*. This category has been used since Mishnaic times.[19] The Traditional texts define what may and may not be done to this person as well as their rights.[20] None of these texts define the time limit of the *goses* precisely; that was done by Joshua Falk, a Polish Talmudist who died in 1614.[21] He defined the period within three days of death basing himself on the statement of Joseph Caro: "When they say that we have seen your relative *goses* for three days, we consider him dead and should mourn him." The definition was in keeping with the medical knowledge of the period although that is difficult to establish for Eastern Europe.

We also need a clear definition of the "end stage of life" and should look at contemporary medical research for it. With the modern technology available to us, it is legitimate to define that stage by specific conditions rather than a time frame. For example, an irreversable coma, brain death, the recognized final painful stages of various forms of cancer, AIDS, Hungtingon's Chorea, and other diseases for which there is neither a cure nor a way of halting the progress of the disease.

When these stages have been reached, we may consider the person a *goses*, and halt all treatment. I would advocate going further and assisting to a painless death.

RESPECT FOR LIFE AND THE GOOD LIFE

Let us continue by discussing the decisions which will face the patient and the family. There is an underlying respect for human life from Biblical times onward. Both the later *halakhic* and *aggadic* traditions clearly demonstrate a respect for life as a Divine gift, as initially expressed in the Genesis story. In that tale it is the Divine breath of life through which "man becomes a living soul." For the rabbis of the Talmud the first commandment of the Bible is "Be fruitful and multiply".

Our love of life must lead to a desire to perpetuate it and so every human must do his/her best to continue it into the next generation. Marriage and procreation have always been high on our agenda[22].

When human life was in danger, every commandment except murder, adultery and idolatry could be trespassed in order to save a human life, Jewish or Gentile. *Piquah nefesh* therefore overrode all other obligations including the stringent restrictions on the Sabbath. Furthermore, all medical efforts must be made by the attending physician and the staff in order to preserve human life. There is a long series of discussions on this matter which stretches from the Talmud to the present day and the answer in every case of true danger is positive.[23]

95

Every human life is to be valued but not necessarily forever. Our technology has enabled us to examine the grey area between life and death, so we must discuss the quality of life. Judaism has been willing to accept suffering when it could not be avoided but has not turned it into a virtue. Sometimes, of course, suffering was seen as a Divine test as in the story of Job. However, that story is a very good example of the dominant view that there is nothing wrong with the enjoyment of life and that, in fact, happiness, which the material and personal aspects of life bring is highly desirable and should be attained by as many people as possible. When Job withstood the test and even Satan, the adversary, was satisfied, everything was restored to Job. He then had twice as much as before; his family life was renewed with seven sons and three daughters; his wealth was impressive and he lived a long life. In other words, the experience had not turned him into an ascetic saint who renounced the world and its pleasures. That might have been expected but it was not the turn which this story took.

There have been ascetics in Jewish history, people who renounced both the pleasures of a personal life as well as those of worldly comfort. They are mentioned in our tradition, sometimes even mildly praised, but they have never become its heroes. That is true of the major Biblical figures, beginning with Abraham and continuing through David and Solomon who were celebrated for worldly success. Various later rabbis combined personal wealth with communal leadership, as Judah Hanasi (second century), Saadia Gaon (ninth century), Hasdai Ibn Shaprut (eleventh century), Meir of Rothenburg (fourteenth century), David Oppenheim, (eighteenth century), and many others. As long as individuals took their personal and communal Jewish responsibility seriously and looked after those who were less fortunate, they were not required to abstain from the joys of material blessings. In other words, a good quality of life has always been seen as a positive goal toward which individuals might well strive alongside the development of their religious character and their intellectual abilities.

Small groups have followed more ascetic paths, usually influenced by the surrounding cultures. They have been duly recorded but never made normative. Furthermore, they did so as a matter of personal choice. We know of the Nazarites of Biblical times, among others.[24] The Essenes and the Qumran sect in the first century isolated themselves, did not marry, and led a very simple life far removed from most of the pleasures of the remainder of the community.[25] In the Middle Ages, the *Hassidim* of Germany were ascetic and engaged in the same kind of practices as some of the neighboring Christian communities. Various days were set aside for fasting as well as for abstinence from sexual relations; among some, a simple life of poverty was advocated. Those patterns occurred at various other times in Jewish history as well, mainly connected with mysticism and the yearning for a union with God or a deeper understanding of the essence of the commandments. The renunciation of much that was this worldly was a way of gaining quality of life in "the other" world of the totally spiritual.

It is interesting to note that although these paths existed and gained some followers in virtually every generation, they have only occasionally attracted the masses, as for example immediately after the destruction of the Temple in 70 C.E. and following the Crusades in the eleventh century.[26] Generally the normative *halakhah* has added such practices as footnotes or as the path of the very pious, not recommended for the ordinary individual. A good, religious, and happy life which sought God, observed the *mitzvot*, cared for the welfare of everyone in the community, and assured a reasonable standard of living, was the goal continually emphasized.

Charitable efforts, therefore, were not aimed solely at alleviating utter poverty and total depravation but also at elevating people's status. The primary effort was to provide employment so that the poor could lift themselves out of poverty and did not lose their dignity and hope for the future. Under some circumstances, loans were encouraged in place of outright gifts. Everyone in each community was charged with these

97

responsibilities.[27] This and a good deal more indicates that the quality of life played a positive role in Judaism, and that a high quality of life was considered a noble goal even if it was not possible in many periods of our history.[28]

Poverty, ill health and persecution were seen as punishment for sins by some theologians, but this rarely led to a feeling that the opposite, the good life was sinful; nor was asceticism and self-depravation seen as the road to "salvation" either for the individual or for the entire community.

The road to the good life included physical health along with all the other blessings. Appropriate words of gratitude are therefore expressed to God for maintaining physical health and all bodily functions in the regular daily morning service. Special thanks are to be given on arising. Prayers of gratitude after recovery from illness are part of the liturgy and of private prayer. There are Biblical verses which point to God as the sole healer and later rabbinic literature occasionally took that position as pointed our earlier. However, the dominant note was, and remains, that everything which can be done to enhance health or to heal the sick should be undertaken. In addition, all that could be done to alleviate pain and suffering was undertaken with few restrictions.

A HUMANE DEATH

Tradition has sought to provide a decent and humane death whenever it was within our hands to do so. For example, when the Talmud dealt with the execution of criminals, it was to be done in a humane manner without mental or physical suffering. Death should be quick. Anything which might lead to psychological suffering was avoided. Everything was done to assure that the execution could be stopped if new evidence arose, but otherwise the sentence was carried out speedily.[29]

As we have taken such precautions with condemned criminals, then we should certainly take similar steps with normal decent people who have simply entrusted themselves to a medical system which may not know when to stop. We must also state that the advance of medical technology has made the distinction between passive and active steps to sustain life meaningless or of doubtful value. We would place them together and argue that as the end approaches no further medical intervention of any kind should take place and we should proceed to a humane death as with those condemned by a court.

MEDICAL ECONOMICS

We also need to look at medical economics, although we may be tempted to state that monetary considerations shall not be permitted to play a role in a decision like end-stage euthanasia. They will play a role and so we need to discuss them frankly. As we look into the realm of medical economics, it is, of course, tempting simply to indicate, along with the Tradition, that all human lives are of equal value and that we cannot make a decision to save one rather than another.

Saving any human life takes precedence over all commandments except murder, incest and idolatry. Neglecting to receive proper medical help is a sin. Every effort must be made even on *Shabbat* to rescue individuals from a collapsed building, etc.[30] Furthermore, if it is possible to save one life out of a number, then one should do so. A passage of the Talmud discussed two individuals who were lost in the desert and did not have sufficient water for both to survive. What should be done? Interestingly enough two contradictory answers were provided. Ben Petura suggested that both should die so that one would not witness the death of his fellow human being, but Akiba stated that "your life takes precedence".[31] This quotation from the Talmud is helpful only as it refused to consider doing nothing. Of course, it does not help us to decide who should be saved.

99

A well known Mishnah in *Ohalot* may be of some slight use. It dealt with a woman, who faced enormous difficulty in giving birth to a child . The physician had to make a decision between saving the woman or allowing the child to be born. The Mishnah indicated that the woman's life was to be saved and the fetus may be dismembered. That was true until the head of the child emerged, then it was considered a person and one could not choose the life of one individual over another. The decision was then left to the physician.[32] Here again we have a statement that both lives are equal unless one has not yet attained the status of a person.

These statements have shown us that a life must be saved and it is our duty to do so, but they do not help us to decide which life to save. These statements are of less use when we are asked to guide legislation and are not dealing with single individuals for whom a decision must be made. Liberal Jewish discussions of this question must begin. In our discussion the larger public good and the Jewish view toward it must be carefully considered. It should be our task to enter this discussion and help to establish appropriate guidelines.

END-STAGE EUTHANASIA

Jewish tradition continues to oppose euthanasia in all instances except the final stage of life. When a person has reached this stage and is suffering, we may consider that individual minimally as a *goses*, but actually need to go further in a direction which will be helpful to the patient and to the family along the lines discussed by my colleagues in their papers.

End-stage euthanasia fits into our understanding of the covenantal relationship with God. It meets the criteria of the Jewish emphasis on a good life and the humane treatment of individuals. We may permit end-stage euthanasia within the confines of the *halakhah*.

Notes

1. *Sanhedrin* 23a; *Yoma* 85b; *Shabbat* 132b; Alfasi, *Shabbat*, ch 5, p. 139b.

2. *Yad, Hil. Avel* 4.5; *Tur* and *Shulhan Arukh, Yoreh Deah* 339.

3. The chief case against active euthanasia was taken from the fate of Haninah ben Teradion, (second century) *(b.* A. Z. 18a) who was burned at the stake, wrapped in a *Torah*, by the Romans for his rebellious act of teaching *Torah*. His disciples wished to ease the process and asked him to open his mouth, so that he would die more quickly, but he refused. They advocated suicide; he refused. On the other hand, when the pagan executioner asked whether he could increase the temperature of the fire and remove sponges, which kept him alive, he agreed. Active help toward death by an outside party was therefore possible with the agreement of the dying party. The executioner acted and when the rabbi had died, jumped into the fire himself. Haninah ben Teradion was unwilling to take steps himself, in other words, to commit suicide, but was willing to permit someone else to hasten the process of death. This path was, however, not discussed further.

4. An elderly woman (*Yalkut Shemoni* Vol. II, # 943) felt that her life had no further meaning and she asked R. Yose Hagalili, whether she could stop praying in the synagogue as she felt that this alone was keeping her alive. He agreed; she stopped her regular prayers and three days later died. There were no negative comments on her path of action.

5. Exodus 15.16; II Chronicles 16.12f; Jeremiah 8.22; Job 13.4.

6. Exodus 21,18f.

7. Leviticus 13, 14; II K 5.1; Ben Sirach 38.1ff and Tobit 2.10.

8. Irene and Walter Jacob, *Pharmaceuticals in the Biblical and Rabbinic World*, Leiden, 1993.

9. *M.* Kid 4.14; *b.* B. K. 46b, 85a; Julius Preuss, *Biblical and Talmudic Medicine* (T. R. Fred Rosner), New York, 1978, pp 11ff.

10. Some letters allude to this attitude, see Jacob Mann, *Texts and Studies in Jewish History and Literature*, Vol. II - *Karaitica*, Philadelphia, 1935. Karaites were more stringent than rabbinic Jews in granting permission to violate the Sabbath for medical emergencies, but in desperate situations, it was permitted. Leon Nemoy, *Karaite Anthology*, New Haven, 1952, pp. 267 ff.

11. Nahmanides to Ex 15.26; 23.25. Ibn Ezra to Ex 21.19.

12. Lev 19.16; Deut 22.1; San 73a; *b. A.Z.* 28b; *b. B. M.* 85b; *b. B. K.* 81b; 85a; *Yad Hil Deah* 3.3; etc.

13. Julius Preuss, *Biblical and Talmudic Medicine,* tr. Fred Rosner, New York, 1970. This is the best general survey of the field.

14. Steven Newmyer, "Asaph the Jew and Greco-Roman Pharmaceutics"; Irene and Walter Jacob, (ed.) *The Healing Past,* pp 107 ff

15. Maimonides, *Medical Treatises,* Vol I, II, III, tr. Fred Rosner, New York, 1970?; Fred Rosner, *Medicine in the Mishneh Torah of Maimonides,* New York, 1984.

16. Wilhelm Ebstein and Benno Jacob, *Die Medizin im Alten Testament,* Stuttgart, 1901; Julius Preuss, *Op. Cit.*; Harry Friedenwald, *Jews and Medicine,* Vol I and II, 1944, Baltimore; this book provides a good bibliography of works in modern European languages as well as a list of Jewish physicians.

17. Letter to Ibn Tibbon, written in 1199.

18. Daniel Jeremy Silver, *Maimonidean Criticism and the Maimonidean Controversy 1180-1240,* Leiden, 1965.

19. *Semahot* 1.3; *M. Oholot* 1.6; *Git.* 28a.

20. *Yad Hil. Avel* 4.5; *Tur* and *Shulhan Arukh, Yoreh Deah* 339 and Isslerles.

21. *Perishah* to *Tur, Yoreh Deah* 339.

22. Genesis 2.7; Genesis 2.8; *b. Kid* 29b; *b. Pes* 49a; *b. Ber.* 16a; *b. Git* 41b; *b. Yeb.* 61b ff; *Yad Hil, Ishot* 15 Tur, *Shulhan Arukh Even Haezer.*

23. Leviticus 18,5; *b. Yoma* 85b; *Shulhan Arukh Orah Hayim* 328.3 ff; 329.3 and Isserles.

24. Nu 6.8; Lev 10.8 ff; 21; I Sam 1.11. There is a tractate of the *Mishnah* devoted to the Nazarites, but we should note that there is no *gemara* on it. Furthermore, some of the Nazarite vows were temporary. All of this was dropped by later rabbinic Judaism. In the Biblical period the Rechabites were also mentioned as an ascetic group, but we know almost nothing about them (Jer. 35, II K 10.15 ff; Neh 3.14 f). In rabbinic literature they were discussed occasionally (*b. B.B.* 92b; *M. Ta-anit* 4.5; *b. Sotah* 11a, *Sifrei* Num. 78, etc.).

25. Josephus, *Antiquities,* XIII 5, 9; XVIII 1,2; B.J. II 8, 2-13; and Philo. For an excellent discussion and bibliography see G. Vermes, F. Millar, M. Black, eds., Emil Schürer, *The History of the Jewish People in the Age of Jesus Christ,* Vol 2, Edinburgh, 1979, pp 555 ff.

102

26. *Travels of Benjamin of Tudela* 2.11, 12; Bahyah Ibn Pakudah placed some emphasis on asceticism. On the other hand, Maimonides vigorously opposed such tendencies (*Yad* Hil Deut. 3.1; 6.1). *Sefer Hassidim* (#433, #990, #1174, #1200) mentioned the ascetic practices of various leaders, among them - Judah Hahasid. Abraham b. David of Posquieres in the thirteenth century along with his followers were ascetic as were others influenced by the *Kabbalah*. We should also note that many Karaite scholars were ascetics (H. Graetz, *Geschichte des Judenthums*, Vol. 3 pp. 417 ff).

27. *b. B. B.* 60b, *Tosefta Sota* - end; *b. Ket* 104b; *Sefer Hassidim*.

28. Yeb 62b; *Sefer Hassidim* #1049 - deal with loans for the poor. Employment was emphasized from Talmudic times onward (*Shab* 63a; *Mak.* 24a; *Yad Hil. Matnat Aniyim* 107f). The systematic arrangements were discussed in some detail (*Yad Hil. Aniyam* 9.1-3; *Shulhan Arukh* 250).

29. *b. San* 45a, - 52a; *b. Pes* 75a; *b. Ket* 37a

30. *Shulhan Arukh, Orah Hayim* 129.4 ff; *Yoma* 83a ff.

31. *b. B. M.* 62a.

32. *M.* Ohlot 7.6; *Shulhan Arukh Hoshen Mishpat* 425.2.

DETERMINING DEATH IN JEWISH LAW*

Moshe Zemer

Determining *halakhic* death is not merely a theoretical issue or academic exercise. Historically, the *halakhic* definition of death has had practical consequences for many matters including marital status, *yibum*, inheritance, euthanasia, homicide and, more recently, organ transplants.

The following example may well illustrate that this is a contemporary issue: A violent argument broke out between a married couple on 16 November, 1982, at 3:45 am in a community near Tel Aviv. The husband put an end to the dispute by throwing his wife out of the window of their fourth floor apartment (the equivalent of the fifth floor in North America). When the victim was brought to Assaf HaRofe Hospital, the attending physicians pronounced her brain dead. They connected her to an artificial respirator and other life support systems.

It took five days to locate the woman's relatives to receive permission to have her kidneys donated to two desperately ill patients. After extracting the kidneys the doctors disconnected the support systems.

The "bereaved" widower was convicted of murder in the first degree by the Tel Aviv District Court. In his appeal to the Israel Supreme Court, the defense attorney put forth an original argument on behalf of his client. The appellant admitted that he threw his wife out of the window, but claimed that it was not he who had killed her. She was still alive in the hospital--her heart was beating and she was breathing as long as she was connected to the life sustaining apparatus-- until the doctors pulled the plug and disconnected her. That's what really killed his wife!

The verdict of the Supreme Court, which includes a learned study on determining death in the *halakhah*, upheld the District Court's conviction and sentence of life imprisonment.[1]

Defining death in Jewish law begins with an entirely different issue: How long must a rescuer continue to desecrate the Shabbat while digging a victim from the debris of a collapsed building? Since *piquah nefesh* (danger to life) overrides virtually all the *mitzvot* including the Shabbath, we must continue to dig away as long as the trapped victim is known or believed to be alive. Once the person is found to be dead, we may no longer violate the Sabbath for him/her.

The *Mishnah Yoma* specifies: "If debris fall on someone, and it is doubtful... whether he is alive or dead...you should clear away the debris from the person [even on *Shabbat*]. If you find him alive, the debris should be removed, but if he be dead, leave him there [until the Shabbat is over]."[2]

The *Gemara* asks: "How far does one search (if the person buried under the debris gives no sign of life? One view is that you search until you reach his nose. The other view is as far as his heart..."[3]

Rashi comments that we search as far as his nose because "if there is no sign of life in his nostrils, (which means, he is not breathing), then he is indeed dead and they may leave him. A contradictory view claims that we should check as far as his heart...to determine whether there is life with his breath pulsing there."[4]

Rav Papa (a fifth generation Babylonian *Amora*) ruled between these two views: "If one has searched as far as the nose, it is not necessary to search any further as is written in Scripture: "In whose nostrils is the breath of the spirit of life." (Genesis 7:22)[5]

This verse reveals that the essential test of existence is the breath of life in one's nostrils. This also appears to be the *peshat* (plain meaning) of the Torah's story of the creation of man: "And the Lord fashioned man of dust of the earth and instilled in his nostrils the breath of life and man became a living creature." (Genesis 2:7) Spontaneous respiration is thus the primary sign of the living state.

Maimonides rules that the *halakhah* in this controversy is according to the *tana kama* (first opinion) of the *beraita (Tannaitic* statement):

> If they examined him as far as his nostrils and found no breath there - they leave him alone because he is already dead.[6]

The *Shulhan Arukh* followed suit:

> Even if they found him crushed and mangled, so that he can live a short while, they clear away the debris and examine him as far as his nose, so if they determine no sign of life there, then he is indeed dead.[7]

BRAIN DEATH

Is there a scientific basis for the *halakhic* determination that the cessation of respiration is the end of life? Yes, indeed. This view of the *halakhah* is related to the most authoritative, modern medical determination of human demise, namely, brain death. The ability to determine a state of brain death is the most widely accepted medical and legal definition of death. It has also advanced the understanding of *halakhic* demise.

In 1968, a special interdisciplinary group of experts was brought together at Harvard University to investigate this problem. It became world renowned as the "*Ad Hoc* Committee of the Harvard Medical School to Examine the Definition of Brain Death." Its report declared: "Our primary purpose is to define irreversible coma as a new criterion of death." The committee set four very thorough neurological examinations to establish brain death, that became known as "the Harvard criteria."

These include:
1. Lack of receptivity and response to external stimuli or internal need.
2. Absence of spontaneous breathing or movement as observed by a physician over a period of at least one hour,
3. Absence of elicitable reflexes,
4. And a flat EEG, i.e., an isoelectric electroencephalogram, in order to confirm the first three.[8]

There is a conflict among certain Orthodox scholars as to whether the Harvard process is acceptable. on the other hand, Rabbi Walter Jacob accepts these recommendations of the Harvard Committee, finding them compatible with the *halakhah*. "We are satisfied that these criteria include those of the older tradition and comply with our concern that life has ended.[9]

How does this scientific determination of brain death relate to the Talmudic criterion of the cessation of respiration? Medical science tells us that the center that controls breathing is located in the medulla oblongata in the brain stem. Some modern *halakhists* claim that the cessation of breathing signifies the death of the brain stem which controls breathing. From this point of view, the halakhic test for death, the cessation of breathing parallels the modern medical test for brain death. The former Chief Rabbi of Israel, Shlomo Goren expressed such a view: "Brain death means the irreversible cessation of all the functions of the brain including the brain stem...I have clearly established that the cessation of respiration of an injured person, when he is in the condition of irreversible brain death, as when breathing through the nose has ceased, constitutes death. This is exactly what we have found in the tractate *Yoma*".[10]

Not every *halakhic* authority has accepted the cessation of breathing as the sole criterion for death.

Rabbi Zvi Ashkenazi, known as Hakham Zvi of Lemberg, (1660-1718) declared that assigning the sign of life to the nostrils alone was too simplistic: "Breathing going from the heart through the lung is recognizable only as long as the heart is alive. It is very clear that there is no respiration except when there is life in the heart." In his view, the heart-beat must serve as an additional criterion for the cessation of life.[11]

Rabbi Moshe Schreiber, the famed Hatam Sofer of Pressburg, Hungary, (1762-1839) stated: "The measure and determination of death were given as Law to Moses on Sinai (*halakhah lemosheh misinai*) "and established three criteria for determining death:

1. The person has been lying still like an inanimate stone,
2. There is no pulse whatsoever
3. And respiration has ceased,
(This means) he is dead and his burial should not be delayed.

The decisor conjectures that "this determination of death might have been a tradition of the first naturalists (*mesorat mibaalei tiviim harishonim*), on whom our rabbinic sages relied in many matters of Torah, but forgotten by today's physicians."[12] Unfortunately, Sofer does not reveal to us the identity of these "first naturalists".

Rabbi Solomon B. Freehof, contrasts the traditional and scientific approaches to determining death. He underlines Moses Sofer's defense of the Jewish custom of immediate burial, on the same day. This custom relies on traditional judgement, embodied in the knowledge of the *Hevra Qadishah* (Burial Society), constituting sufficient proof of death. Freehof claims that modern scientific opinions are much stricter than Jewish tradition in determining when a potential donor is actually dead.[13]

109

Rabbi Shlomo Goren claims that the above responsum by the Hatam Sofer establishes only one criterion for death: the cessation of breathing. "The other two are merely an expression of the condition of the irreversible cessation of breathing, namely brain death, including the brain stem.[14] As we shall see, some contemporary rabbinic scholars disagree with this interpretation resulting in a severe *halakhic* controversy.

SCHOLARLY VIEWS OF THE MEANING OF HUMAN LIFE AND DEATH

Professors of medicine and law have interpreted the process of determining death as more than a medical or legal issue.

A foremost legal savant declared: "In reconsidering the definition of death, the medical profession has determined that death is a process rather than an event. Recent medical achievements in artificially prolonging life have led physicians to conclude that patients reach a stage in the process of dying beyond which no chance for recovery exists. The cessation of total brain function known as brain death, is widely accepted as constituting an irreversible stage in the process of dying beyond which all other organs imminently will cease to function."[15]

Scholars of the *Journal of the American Medical Association* stated:

The principal reason for deciding that a person is dead should be based on a fundamental understanding of the nature of man... Without a brain, the body becomes the convenient medium in which the energy-requiring states of organs run down and the organs decay. These residual activities (of organs without nervous system influence) do not confer an iota of humanity or personality. Thus in the circumstance of brain death neither a human being nor a person any longer exists... Almost all segments of society will agree that some capacity to think, to perceive, to respond and to regulate and integrate bodily functions is essential to human nature. Thus, if none of these brain functions are present nor will they ever return, it is no longer appropriate to consider a person as a whole as being alive.[16]

Expressions of this sort are rarely, if ever, found in *halakhic* literature, where human life or death are empirical issues.

DECAPITATION

There is an additional *halakhic* explanation of brain death other than that of the cessation of respiration.

In the Mishnah[17], we learn that if the head of an animal is cut off, it becomes unclean, (as a dead creature), even if its limbs continue to quiver, just like the lizard whose tail still twitches (after it is cut off).

Dr. Moshe Tendler, son-in-law of Rabbi Moshe Feinstein, explains that the authorities of Jewish Law considered the decapitated individual dead immediately upon severance of the spinal cord although cardiac function had not ceased. The residual life is considered to be without ethical import "like the twitching of a lizard's amputated tail." (*M. Ohalot* 1.6) It would follow logically that irreversible loss of spontaneous respiration due to interruption of blood flow to the brain stem is tantamount to a physiologic decapitation.[18]

IS ORGAN TRANSPLANTING *HALAKHICALLY* PERMISSIBLE?

What is the *halakhic* and practical significance of brain death today? Of all of the areas of Jewish medical ethics, perhaps its definition is most crucial for organ transplanting.

111

Human organ transplantation of various kinds have been successfully performed for four decades. The first heart transplant took place in Capetown in 1963. Since then there have been lung, heart, liver and other organ transplants in many parts of the world including Israel. In the beginning of each new surgical transplant procedure there was a high mortality rate among the recipients.

At the end of the 1960's, Rabbi Moshe Feinstein of New York and Israel Chief Rabbi Yehudah Unterman proclaimed that heart transplants were tantamount to double murder of both the donor and the recipient. The donors were not considered dead before the extraction of the organ. A very large percentage of recipients died shortly after surgery.[19]

In 1976, Feinstein wrote a responsum to his son-in-law, Rabbi Prof. Moshe Tendler, of the Departments of Biology and Talmudic Law at Yeshiva University, stating that he had revised his position on brain death. Prof. Tendler had informed him that it had become possible to determine by various tests that there was no longer any connection between brain and body, the brain had already been completely destroyed and would be considered like a decapitated person... once the death of the person has occurred and can be determined, there is no *halakhic* obligation to maintain treatment or artifical support of the corpse. Thus, according to Moshe Feinstein, there is no religious imperative to continue to use a respirator to inflate and deflate the lungs and thus maintain the cellular viability of other organs in an otherwise dead patient.[20]

The next step to permit extraction of donor organs for transplants was not far away. And indeed the Israel Chief Rabbinate Council reached a decision on brain death and heart transplants a brief ten years later on November 30, 1986.

The decision included the following points:
"In the last decade several fundamental medical changes affecting heart transplants have taken place:

a.   The survival rate has risen. Approximately 80% of heart transplant recipients now survive at least one year (*hayei olam*, namely, long term life) and approximately 70% survive five years.

b.   It is possible today to confirm in an absolutely reliable and secure manner that cessation of respiration in a dying person is final and irreversible.

c.   Evidence has been brought before us that even Rabbi Moshe Feinstein, in later years, permitted heart transplant procedures in the United States [thereby reversing his previously negative position].

d.   Based upon the Talmudic principles of *Yoma* 85, and ruled according to Hatam Sofer, the *halakhah* holds that death occurs with the cessation of respiration. Therefore one must confirm that respiration has ceased completely and irreversibly.

e.   The medical-rabbinic committee must follow certain procedures and guidelines to confirm the brain death of the donor [which include the Harvard criteria and additional tests].[21]

Thus heart transplants were made possible from a religious-*halakhic* point of view as well as medically.

SHORT TERM VS. LONG TERM LIFE: *HAYEI OLAM VE-HAYEI SHA'AH*

A crucial *halakhic* issue is whether to endanger the short term life (*hayei shaah*, literally, "life of the hour") of the dangerously ill recipient of the organ transplant if this surgical action will increase his longevity (*hayei olam*, or long term life). At a time of certain danger, we do not pay attention to the short term as long as there is the slightest chance of prolonging his life.

113

A physician asked R. Yaakov Reischer (1670-1733, Austria) about a patient who was near death. All his doctors gave him but a day or two to live. However, they believed that there was another medicine which may cure him or possibly the opposite, for if he takes the medicine and it does not succeed, Heaven forbid, (*has vehalilah*) he will die within an hour or two. Is it permissible to give him this drug or are we concerned for his short term life so that it would be preferable to take no action? R. Reischer replied: If it is possible that he may be completely cured by means of this medicine, then we are not concerned about his short term life.[22]

R. Reischer's verdict is based on a *sugya* in the Talmud: "Raba said in the name of R. Johanan: In the case where it is doubtful whether the patient will live or die, we most not allow gentile physicians to heal; but if he will certainly die, there is still the life of the hour [*hayei shaah*] (to be considered). [The conclusion of the gemara is:] The life of the hour is not to be considered."[23]

ULTRA-ORTHODOX OPPOSITION

Not all of the traditionalists agree with the Chief Rabbinate's decision on brain death and heart transplants.

R. Shlomo Zalman Auerbach, one of the foremost Orthodox rabbinic authorities in Israel met with Dr. Avraham Sofer Avraham, the head of internal medicine at Jerusalem's Sha'arei Zedek Hospital. This physician, who is also an Orthodox rabbi, explained the medical aspects of brain death to him. Auerbach replied:

> You have convinced me that in most cases a patient like this (whose brain is irreversibly damaged) will die in an extremely short period of time. However, there is no evidence at all that he is dead now. In any event as long as his heart is beating, it is forbidden to do anything that

will hasten his death. In order to establish death you must prove the absence of all three conditions (set by the Hatam Sofer: an inanimate body, no pulse and no breathing)... Since there is no definition (of brain stem death) in the Talmud, we cannot invent a new definition in our time. Only when the *Sanhedrin* will be established, will we have the power to determine whether brain stem death is considered death or not. Until then, he said, it is forbidden to extract his heart or any other organ as long as his heart is beating.[24]

R. Auerbach and another ultra-orthodox colleague, Rabbi Yosef Elyashiv published the following proclamation on 18 Menahem Av, 5751 (29 July, 1991):

Behold, any time that the donor's heart is beating, even in the case that his entire brain, including the brain stem, is not functioning at all, which is called 'brain death', our judgement is that there is no *heiter* (no permission) whatsoever to remove any of his organs; doing so is a form of murder."

(Rabbi) Shlomo Zalman Auerbach   (Rabbi) Yosef Elyashiv

Auerbach strictly forbids disconnecting a brain death patient from life supporting systems:

In our day if a patient is still connected to the artificial respirator which doesn't allow him to die, his *halakhic* position is that part of him is alive since his heart is beating, even though this is only because of the respirator..."[25]

Eliezer Yehudah Waldenberg, a member of the *Bet Hadin*

115

Harabbani Hagadol, (the Supreme Rabbinic Court which is part of Israel's religious establishment) is considered the foremost respondent on *halakhah* and medicine today. In a learned responsum he gives a medico-historical survey of determining death:

> The sages of the nations disagreed whether the life of every living creature depends on the brain or the heart. Claudius Galenus (the Greek physician of the second century B.C.E) determined that it is dependent on the brain. Aristotle reasoned the opposite that everything depends on the heart. Then came the great teacher and physician, our Rabbi the Rambam *z"l*, and decided according to the view of Aristotle that life depends on the heart, and as long as there is a sign of life in it, this creature has a status of a living person.

Waldenberg proceeds with a severe critique of modern medical science and physicians for their contrary views, and particularly, the introduction of "so-called brain death":

> The intention of these doctors is to make changes in matters which our Holy Sages have established. No power exists which may change them at all. (These scientists') revelations and learned articles stand in contradiction to *hazal*. We know by virtue of innumerable *experiments* from ancient times until today that medical proclamations and revelations are not always "the last word". Whatever was determined to be true medicine, was afterwards disregarded as useless, or even harmful.

In contrast to R. Goren, he interprets Hatam Sofer literally:

In addition to the cessation of the functions of the brain,

116

even in its entirety, we need, according to the *halakhah*, in order to determine brain death, also the absence of breathing and the absence of heart function including the lack of pulse and activity."[26]

We see that Orthodox *halakhic* pluralism exists in Israel. Those who are in favor of religious pluralism might see this is as a positive step forward. However, the result is a severe obstacle to organ transplants. What is the reason?

Israel has excellent surgical teams. It has the Chief Rabbinate's decision which gave their *hekhsher* in 1986. However, there is a drastic shortage of donor organs. Unfortunately, Israel has a very high mortality rate from automobile and other accidents which result in head injuries and brain death. Desperately ill people, Jews and Arabs, are waiting for a heart or liver or other organ which will save them from certain death. The physicians turn to the family of the fatally injured for permission to donate the organ. Rabbis like Auerbach, Elyashiv, Waldenberg and their followers are constantly preaching and publishing their view that giving permission to extract an organ from their beloved dead is murder.

Mourning often involves religious regression. Relatives of the deceased, who are not orthodox or even traditional, may at this time of tragedy be influenced by such *halakhic* and theological harassment. The family may be subject to implantation of fear and guilt that they are murdering their beloved and disobeying God's commands. The result is that they refuse to allow the transplant. This refusal is a death warrant for the ill. In spite of all the progress with transplantation, with life support systems and the ability to determine a state of brain death and to find *halakhic* justification for each step, extremist religious groups are interfering with the process of saving human lives.

In the Talmud, we are told that if you see your neighbor drowning, mauled by beasts or attacked by robbers, you are bound to save the person--even at the cost of your own life.[27]

It would seem that *kal vehomer (a fortiori)* reasoning may resolve the question before us: How much the more must the organ of a brain dead person be donated to save a human life.[28]

Notes

* Dedicated to the memory of Sergeant Jonathan Boyden, who fell in battle in Lebanon, July, 1993.

1. (Judge) M. Beisky, Supreme Court Criminal Appeal 341/82, Nathan Blacker v. the State of Israel, *Supreme Court Verdicts,* vol. 41, part 1, 1987. Among the many legal precedents supporting this verdict, the jurist quotes (on page 28) a similar case: "The death resulted not from turning off the respirator, but from the defendant's acts, which undeniably caused the victim's brain to die. Having caused 'brain death', the defendant was properly found criminally responsible for homicide." (State of New Jersey v. Watson 467 A 2d., 1983, p. 591.

2. *Mishnah Yoma* 8:6

3. *b. Yoma* 5a *beraita*

4. Rashi, *ad loc., s.v. ad hotmo*

5. *b. Yoma* 85a

6. Laws of *Shabbat* 2:19

7. *Shulhan Arukh Orah Hayim* 329.4

8. "*Ad Hoc* Committee of the Harvard Medical School to Examine the Definition of Brain Death." JAMA, Chicago, 1968, v. 205, p. 337.

9. Walter Jacob, *Contemporary American Responsa,* ed., New York, 1987, no. 78, pp. 130-131.

10. *Hatzofe,* Tel Aviv, 21 August, 1992

11. R. Zevi Ashkenazi, *Responsa Hakham Zvi,* Jerusalem, 1970, no. 77, p. 40a.

12. R. Moshe Sofer, *Responsa Hatam Sofer, Yoreh Deah*, Vienna, 1983, no. 338

13. *American Reform Responsa,* (ed.) Walter Jacob, CCAR, New York, 1983, no. 86, p. 292

14. *Harefuah*, Vol. 122, part 4, 16.2.92, p. 263

15. P. L. Ryan, "The Uniform Determination of the Death Act: An Effective Solution to the Problem of Defining Death," *Washington & Lee Law Review*, vol. 39, 1982, p. 1512.

16. Frank J. Veith, *JAMA*, Oct. 10, 1977, Vol. 238, # 15, p. 1653.

17. *M. Ohalot* 1:6

18. Moshe D. Tendler, "Cessation of Brain Function: Ethical Implications in Terminal Care and Organ Transplant," *Annals of the New York Academy of Sciences*, ed., Julkus Korein, New York, 1978, pp. 394-395. Similarly, *The Journal of The American Medical Association* explains that complete and irreversible destruction of the brain, which includes loss of all its function can be considered physiological decapitation and thus a determinant *per se* of death. See *JAMA supra* note 16, p. 1654.

19. M. Feinstein, *Responsa Iggrot Moshe Yoreh Deah.* II, no. 74; Y. Unterman, "Problems of Heart Transplants in Light of the Halakhah," *Noam*, vol. 13, pp. 3-9.

20. M. Feinstein, *Op. Cit.* Yoreh Deah III, no. 132 (written communication, 15 May, 1976).

21. "Heart Transplants in Israel".....

22. *Responsa Shevut Yaakov*

23. *b. Avodah Zarah* 27b.

24. Avraham Sofer Avraham, *Nishmat Avraham*, Jerusalem, 1992, Vol. 4, # 339, p. 139.

25. *Ibid.*

26. *Responsa Tzitz Eliezer*, Vol. 17, # 66.

27. *b. Sanhedrin* 73a.

28. This paper was presented in part at the 10th World Congress of Medicine and Law in Jerusalem, 1994.

SELECTED REFORM RESPONSA

These responsa are a representative selection on death and euthanasia chosen from more than a thousand Reform responsa published in the twentieth century. We are grateful to the Central Conference of American Rabbis Press, the Hebrew Union College Press, and Dvir Publishers for permission to reproduce them.

EUTHANASIA (1950)

Israel Bettan

QUESTION: At the convention of the Central Conference of American Rabbis, held in Kansas City, Missouri, 1948, the following resolution emanating from the Commission on Justice and Peace, was adopted:

> This Conference notes that a committee of two thousand physicians in the State of New York has drafted a bill for presentation to the New York Legislature seeking to legalize the practice of orderly scientific euthanasia. We recommend that a special committee of the Conference be appointed to study this important question in the light of Jewish teaching and to bring in a report at the next meeting.*

ANSWER: To carry out the mandate of this resolution, the President of the Conference appointed a committee consisting of the Committee on Responsa and Rabbis Abram V. Goodman and Leon Fram. This committee submits the following report:

Neither in its theoretical nor in its practical aspects does euthanasia present anything new. Among certain primitive peoples, as Westermarck has pointed out, some form of euthanasia has always been prevalent. In ancient Greece, euthanasia was countenanced in some city states, and in Sparta it was rigidly practiced by the state itself. Plato and Aristotle, we know, endorsed it in principle. In the Renaissance period, no less important a person than Sir Thomas More advocated the practice of euthanasia in its voluntary form. He made special provision for it in his *Utopia*. In modern times, during the brief rule of the Nazis, systematic euthanasia, involving the lives of the "useless" and the incurably ill, was authorized by the head of the State and prosecuted with customary ruthlessness (*New Republic*, May 5, 1941; William Shirer, *Berlin Diary*, pp. 454-459).

It is a curious but incontrovertible fact that the theory of euthanasia, even in its most restricted construction, has never invaded

Jewish thought, though "sufferance is the badge of our tribe." In the history of our people, from remotest antiquity to days most recent, we come upon pages that tell of men in agony and despair turning to self-destruction for relief. We also read of men in high places counseling their followers, when faced with sure defeat by a cruel enemy, to welcome self-inflicted death rather than to submit to capture and disgrace. But nowhere do we encounter the suggestion that such examples merit praise and emulation.

The Bible, which affirms religious doctrine more often by implication than by direct command, leaves no doubt as to what the religious man's attitude toward a life of affliction should be. He will accept the lot apportioned to him. He surely will not tamper with the life given him. When Job's wife, herself prostrate at the sight of her husband's overwhelming affliction, cried out, "Dost thou still hold fast to thine integrity? Blaspheme God, and die," Job indignantly replied, "Thou speakest as one of the impious women speaketh. What? Shall we receive good at the hand of God, and shall we not receive evil?" (Job 2:9-10).

Later, in the early Rabbinic period, the same religious temper was evidenced by a famous rabbi who suffered martyrdom for his religious convictions. When Hananiah ben Teradion, a Tannaitic teacher of the second century, was condemned by the Romans to be burned at the stake, his disciples counseled him, as the fires began to flare, to let the consuming flames surge into his frame and thus put a speedy end to his suffering. In reply, the celebrated martyr is reported to have said: "It is best that He Who hath given the soul should also take it away; let no man hasten his own death" (*Avoda Zarah* 18a).

Both of these statements, while seemingly made in a casual manner, were by no means the stray utterances of individual teachers; they sprang from a common ethical tradition. They are closely related to a principle of faith that lies at the foundation of Jewish ethics. Human life is more than a biological phenomenon; it is the gracious gift of God;

it is the inbreathing of His spirit. Man is more than a minute particle of the great mass known as society; he is the child of God, created in His image. "The spirit of God hath made me," avers Job in the midst of his suffering, "and the breath of the Almighty gives me life" (Job 33:4). Thus, human life, coming from God, is sacred, and must be nurtured with great care. And man, bearing the divine image, is endowed with unique and hidden worth and must be treated with reverence.

This principle - which is basic to Judaism, and to which we probably owe whatever spiritual progress that has been made through the centuries - finds clear embodiment in the *halakhah*, in Rabbinic law. The Rabbis were no inflexible legalists; they recognized that not under all circumstances could we condemn unfeelingly the man who chose the way of self-destruction to escape from his hard lot. Yet in formulating the law, they proved uncompromising. The formal rites of mourning, they declared, shall be suspended in the case of one of sound and mature mind who deliberately and of his own volition has laid violent hands on himself; only those rites may be performed the omission of which would give undue offense to the bereaved family (*Semahot* 2.1-5). Likewise, in the case of one who is in dying condition, the law prohibits anyone else from employing any positive and direct means to hasten his death, no matter from what protracted an ailment he may suffer (*Shulhan Arukh, Yoreh Deah* 339). To abridge in some positive and direct manner the duration of life by a single second is tantamount to the shedding of blood (*Shab.* 151b).

Yet Rabbinic law sanctions the use of indirect and negative means to facilitate a peaceful death, such as the elimination of noise and the withholding of stimulants (*Yoreh Deah* 339; *Avodah Zarah* 18a). In the eyes of the law, the causes which may retard the natural process and thus delay the moment of death are artificial, and may therefore be removed. Not so, however, when that which is withheld is a natural physical requirement and essential to sustain life. No nourishment, however little the amount required, may be denied a dying patient whose condition seems hopeless and his pain great, in order to hasten his death (*Tel Talpiyot*, Letter 42, vol. 30, Budapest, 1923).

Of course, we liberal rabbis have always claimed the right, in the interest of a progressive faith, to modify Rabbinic law and to remove what we regard as an obstacle in the advance of the spirit. And, indeed, we have eliminated many an old restriction which, though meant to safeguard Judaism, proved to obscure its essential nature. But we have never sought to nullify an effective Rabbinic implementation of a vital spiritual principle.

The Jewish ideal of the sanctity of human life and the supreme value of the individual soul would suffer incalculable harm if, contrary to the moral law, men were at liberty to determine the conditions under which they might put an end to their own lives and the lives of other men.

*Walter Jacob ed., *American Reform Responsa*, New York, 1983, #78.

EUTHANASIA (1980)

Walter Jacob

QUESTION: A patient has terminal cancer and has sunk into a deep coma. Only the artificial life support systems are keeping him alive. Would Jewish tradition permit these systems to be shut off? What is the Jewish attitude toward euthanasia? (Dr. N.H., Philadelphia, PA)*

ANSWER: Jewish tradition makes a clear distinction between, on the one hand, positive steps which may hasten death, and on the other hand, avoiding matters which may hinder a peaceful end to life. It is clear from the Decalogue (Ex. 21:14; Deut. 5:17) that any kind of murder is prohibited. The only Biblical case of euthanasia was King Saul (I Sam. 31:1ff; II Sam. 1:5ff), who asked his servant to slay him after his own attempt at suicide failed (II Sam. 1:5ff).

In the *Tannaitic* period, the *Mishnaic* tractate *Semahot* (1.1) considered a dying person (*goses*) as a living individual in every respect. That point of view has been followed by later codes such as Maimonides' *Yad* and Caro's *Shulhan Arukh*. It is clear from the *Mishnaic* statement that none of the acts usually performed upon the dead should be done to the dying, nor should a coffin be prepared or matters of inheritance be discussed. The additional later discussion made it clear that no positive acts which may hasten death were to be undertaken, so the *Sefer Hasidim* (723) stated that an individual should not be moved to a different place even if that might make dying easier.

It is further quite clear that we must use any medicine or drug which may help an individual. All *Shabbat* laws may be trespassed to save a life (*Yoma* 85a; *Shulhan Arukh, Orah Hayim* 196.2, 319.17; Ex. 31:14; Lev. 18:5), and even the death of an individual who is seriously ill should not be hastened (*Shulhan Arukh, Yoreh Deah* 339.1). In all these instances, some vague hope remained. However, these injunctions were modified with a dying individual (*goses*) in the throes of death. In that case, it was considered appropriate for an individual to stop praying for the lives of those dear to him or pray for their release (*Ket.* 104a; *Ied.* 40a; *Rema* to *Shulhan Arukh, Even Haezer* 121.7 and *Hoshen*

Mishpat 221.2). Furthermore, it was thought appropriate to stop acts which would hinder the soul from a departure, so *Sefer Hasidim* (723) stated that if a dying person was disturbed by wood chopping, it should be halted so that the soul might depart peacefully. Isserles (to *Shulhan Arukh, Yoreh Deah* 339.1) stated that anything which stood in the way of peaceful death should be removed. Solomon Eger, in his commentary to the same passage of the *Shulhan Arukh*, stated that one should also not use medicine to hinder the soul's departure; he based himself on *Beit Yaakov* (50). Clearly, as long as some form of independent life persists, nothing should be done to hasten death and all medicines which may be helpful must be used. Once this point has been passed, it is no longer necessary to utilize further medical devices in the form of drugs or mechanical apparatus.

We must now attempt to define the turning point, when "independent life" has ceased, and we can best do so by looking carefully at the Jewish and modern medical criteria of death. The traditional criteria were based on a lack of respiratory activity and heart beat (*M. Yoma* 8.5; *Yad, Hil. Shab.* 2.19; *Shulhan Arukh, Orah Hayim* 329.4). Lack of respiration alone was considered conclusive if the individual lay as quietly as a stone *(Responsa Hatam Sofer, Yoreh Deah, #38)*. All of this was discussed at some length in connection with the provision of the *Shulhan Arukh* that an attempt be made to save the child of a woman dying in childbirth; even on *Shabbat* a knife might be brought to make an incision in the uterus in order to remove the fetus (*Shulhan Arukh, Orah Hayim* 330.5). This statement, however, conflicted with the prohibition against moving a limb of someone who was dying, lest that hasten the death (*Shulhan Arukh, Yoreh Deah* 339.1). If one waited until death was absolutely certain, then the fetus would also be dead.

Absolute certainty of death, according to the *halakhic* authorities of the last century, had occurred when there had been no movement for at least fifteen minutes (*Gesher Hayim* I, 3, p. 48) or an hour (*Responsa Yismach Lev, Yoreh Deah, #9*) after the halt of respiration and heart beat. On the other hand, a recent Israeli physician, Jacob Levy, has stated that modern medical methods change this criterion, and the lack of blood pressure as well as respiratory activity should suffice (*Hamaayan, Tamuz*, 5731).

This discussion was, of course, important in connection with the preparation for burial, as well as other matters. When death was certain, then the preparation for burial had to begin immediately (*Hatam Sofer, Yoreh Deah* 338; Azulai's *Responsa Hayim Shaul* II, #25). In ancient times it was considered necessary to examine the grave after a cave burial to be certain that the individual interred had actually died. This was recommended for a period of three days (*Semahot* 8.1). This procedure was not followed after Mishnaic times.

In the last years, it has been suggested that Jews accept the criteria of death set by the *ad hoc* committee of the Harvard Medical School, which examined the definition of brain death in 1968 (*Journal of the American Medical Association*, vol. 205, pp. 337ff). They recommended three criteria: (1) lack of response to external stimuli or to internal need; (2) absence of movement and breathing as observed by physicians over a period of at least one hour; (3) absence of elicitable reflexes; and a fourth criterion to confirm the other three, (4) a flat or isoelectric electroencephalogram. They also suggested that this examination be repeated after an interval of twenty-four hours. Several Orthodox authorities have accepted these criteria, while others have rejected them. Moses Feinstein felt that they could be accepted along with shutting off the respirator briefly in order to see whether independent breathing was continuing (*Igerot Mosheh, Yoreh Deah* II, #174). Moses Tendler has gone somewhat further and has accepted the Harvard criteria (*Journal of the American Medical Association*, vol. 238, #15, pp. 165.1ff). Although David Bleich (*Hapardes, Tevet* 5737) and Jacob Levy (*Hadarom, Nisan* 5731, *Tishri* 5730; *Noam*, 5.30) have vigorously rejected this criterion, we can see that although the question has not been resolved by our Orthodox colleagues, some of them have certainly accepted the recommendations of the Harvard Medical School committee. We are satisfied that these criteria include those of the older tradition and comply with our concern that life has ended. Therefore, when circulation and respiration only continue through mechanical means, as established by the above-mentioned tests, then the suffering of the patient and his/her family may be permitted to cease, as no "natural independent life" functions have been sustained.

We would not endorse any positive steps leading toward death. We would recommend pain-killing drugs which would ease the remaining days of a patient's life.

We would *reject* any general endorsement of euthanasia, but where all "independent life" has ceased and where the above-mentioned criteria of death have been met, further medical support systems need not be continued.

*Walter Jacob ed., *American Reform Responsa,* New York, 1983, #79.

QUALITY OF LIFE AND EUTHANASIA

Walter Jacob

QUESTION: Does Jewish tradition recognize the "quality of life" as a factor in determining medical and general care to preserve and prolong life? I have four specific cases in mind. In the first the patient is in a coma, resides in a nursing home and has not recognized anyone for several years. In the second, the patient is in a nursing home, completely paralyzed and can not speak or make his wishes known in any way. The third is a victim of a stroke, sees no hope for recovery or even major improvement, wishes to die and expresses this wish constantly to anyone who visits. The fourth is slowly dying of cancer, is in great pain and wants a prescription which will relieve her of pain but will probably also slightly hasten death. All of these patients are in their early eighties; none is receiving any unusual medical attention. Should we hope for a new medical discovery which will help them? (Rabbi R. H. Lehman, New York, NY)*

ANSWER: The considerations which govern euthanasia have been discussed by the Committee in a recent responsa (W. Jacob ed., *American Reform Responsa, #79*, 1980). The conclusion of that responsum stated:

> We would not endorse any positive steps leading toward death. We would recommend pain-killing drugs which would ease the remaining days of a patient's life.
>
> We would reject any general endorsement of euthanasia, but where all 'independent life' has ceased and where the above-mentioned criteria of death have been met, further medical support systems need not be continued.

The question here goes somewhat further as we are not dealing with life threatening situations, but with the general question of prolonging life when its quality may be questionable. In none of these situations has any current extraordinary medical attention been provided. In two of the cases the cognitive and/or communicative ability seems to have ended. In the third there is a strong wish for death. In the fourth, the primary concern is relief from pain. Let us look at each of these cases individually.

For the patient in a coma and the one completely paralyzed and unable to communicate, a segment of the brain which provides intelligence seems to be damaged beyond repair. Judaism does not define human life only in terms of mental activity. Every person has been created in the image of God (Gen. 1.26), and so even those individuals who may be defective, i . e . the retarded, the blind, the deaf, the mute, etc., have always been considered as equally created in the image of God; their life is as precious as any other. It is necessary to guard their life and protect it just as any other human life. This is also true of an elderly individual who has now lost some of her mental ability or power of communication. In fact, we owe a special duty toward these individuals who are weak and more likely to be neglected by society just as to the orphan, the widow and the poor (Deut. 14.29, 27.13, Jer. 7.6; Is. 1.17; *Shab.* 133b; *Meg.* 31a; *San* 74a; *Yoma* 82b).

Let us turn to the individual who seeks death and constantly reiterates his wish to die. Although some rabbinic authorities feel that neither an individual nor his family may pray for his death (Haim Palagi *Hiskei Lev,* Vol. 1, *Yoreh Deah* #50), most of our tradition would agree that a person may ask God to be relieved of suffering. The decision, of course, lies with God. A servant of Judah Hanasi prayed for his release (*Ket.* 104a). Other ancient authorities pointed to similar examples (*Ned.* 40a and Commentaries). We would, however, discourage the individual from such prayer and rather seek to encourage a different attitude toward life. The growing field of psychology for the aged has succeeded in developing a variety of techniques for dealing with such long term depression. We would encourage the family and the patient to utilize these methods or any other form of counseling and therapy available.

The individual who seeks relief from her pain should receive drugs which may help, even though they may slightly hasten death. As this is a very long term process, the drug cannot be seen as actually causing her death. Suffering itself has never been seen as an independent good by Judaism. Even criminals destined for execution were drugged to alleviate their suffering (*San.* 43a). Similarly the executioner of the martyr Hanina ben Teradyon was permitted by him to increase the temperature and remove wool sponges from his heart in order to make death a little easier, though Hanina was unwilling to pray for his own death as his disciples suggested (*A. Z.* 18a). We would, therefore, see no objection to relieving the suffering of the woman who is dying from cancer and for whom the drugs are not life threatening.

It is clear that in each of these cases, and in others like them, we should do our best to enhance the quality of life and to use whatever means modern science has placed at our disposal for this purpose. We need not invoke "heroic" measures to prolong life, nor should we hesitate to alleviate pain, but we can also not utilize a "low quality" of life as an excuse for hastening death.

We cannot generalize about the "quality of life" but must treat each case which we face individually. All life is wonderful and mysterious. The human situation, the family setting and other factors must be carefully analyzed before a sympathetic decision can be reached.

December 1985

*Walter Jacob, *Contemporary American Reform Responsa*, New York, 1987, # 83.

HUNTINGTON'S DISEASE AND SUICIDE

Walter Jacob

QUESTION: I am writing about a young woman who has been definitely diagnosed as having Huntington's Disease (sometimes called Huntington's Chorea). It is a genetic disease which is incurable and results in inevitable, severe neurological deterioration causing loss of mental and physical facilities. She has told me that she is contemplating taking her own life when she feels that the disease will rob her of control over her own life and before she deteriorates completely. She asks what would be the Jewish response to her decision? (Rabbi J. Miller, Rochester, NY)*

ANSWER: All of the material relevant to this question has been presented in previous responsa directed toward slightly different questions; the answers were provided by Israel Bettan, Solomon B. Freehof, and Walter Jacob (*American Reform Responsa* ed., #76 ff). In each instance, the writer of the responsum felt that despite the severe problems involved, euthanasia could not be encouraged. This would be equally true of suicide here.

The path of this disease is clearly known and the degenerative affects are terrible, both for the individual involved and those dear to her. Although we can empathize with her wish to commit suicide, it would be difficult for us to approve of this act as Judaism has and continues to object strongly to suicide. The problems which arise under slightly different conditions with other diseases or other circumstances do not make it possible for us to assent to her wish, but we understand it.

June 1983

*Walter Jacob, *Contemporary Reform Responsa*, New York, 1987, # 81.

CAESAREAN ON A DEAD MOTHER

Solomon B. Freehof

QUESTION: A mother eight months pregnant has died. Does Jewish law permit a Caesarean to be performed on her body to save the child? Or, perhaps even more: Does Jewish tradition recommend or urge such an operation? (Asked by Dr. Thomas H. Redding through Rabbi Leonard S. Zoll. Cleveland, Ohio)*

ANSWER: The question of cutting open the body of a mother who has died in order to remove and thus save the child is discussed as far back as the Talmud itself in *Arahin* 7a (cf. also *B.B.* 142b and *Nidah* 44a). The discussion is based upon the Mishnaic law dealing with a pregnant woman who is condemned to death. Do we delay execution of the sentence until she has given birth or not? In the development of that discussion, Rabbi Samuel (*Arahin*) extends the discussion from that of a convicted criminal to any woman who dies when she is near to giving birth ("a woman on the *mashber*, the birth-stool, who dies"). In such circumstances, Rabbi Samuel says that we may bring a knife even on the Sabbath (bringing a knife on the Sabbath is forbidden generally), and we may cut open her body to save the child. The discussion there in the Talmud involves the question of whether the child is alive or not, and the opinion is expressed that generally the child dies immediately (or even before) the mother, and therefore the Sabbath would be violated (by bringing the instruments) in vain, since the child is already dead. But Rashi says: Even in the case of the "doubtful saving of life," we may violate the Sabbath; and therefore, on the chance that the child may be alive, we bring the knife and perform the operation.

It is exactly in this form that the law is recorded by the great legalist and physician, Moses Maimonides, in his *Yad Hilhot Shabbat* 2.15. He says: We perform the operation even on the Sabbath, for even when there is doubt whether we are saving a life, we may violate the Sabbath (cf. also *Tur, ibid.*, and Ephraim Margolis, *Yad Efrayim* to *Orah Hayim* 320).

A new ground for doubt arises, however, in the *Shulhan Arukh* (besides the doubt of violating the Sabbath in vain if the child is already dead). In *Orah Hayim* 330.4, Joseph Caro gives the law according to the Talmud and Maimonides; but Moses Isserles (Poland, 16th century) says: We do not do this operation nowadays because we are no longer skilled in determining precisely whether the mother is dead or not; perhaps she is alive (that is, in coma) and may give birth to the child naturally. However, Isserles himself in his *Responsa* does not seem concerned with this doubt (that the mother may still be alive), and in his Responsum #40 he answers in the affirmative - that is, that the operation should be performed.

As for the later authorities, they all are practically unanimous in favor of permitting the operation (even on the Sabbath, and certainly on week days). What concerns these later authorities is whether or not the permission to perform this operation after the mother is dead may not imply the larger permission for autopsy in general, which Jewish law forbids, except under special circumstances. Generally speaking, it is not permitted to mutilate (*lenavel*) the body of the dead. Therefore, in a discussion between Moses Schick of Ofen and Jacob Ettlinger of Hamburg (both in the first half of the 19th century), this matter is debated (see *Responsa* of Ettlinger, *Binyan Tziyon* 1.171). Moses Schick said in this discussion (in his *Responsa, Yoreh Deah* 347) that we may mutilate the body of a woman to save her child, and Ettlinger says that this permission does not justify general mutilation (as in autopsy) because this operation (that is, the Caesarean) is not really a disfiguring of the body of the woman.

Moses Kunitz (of Budapest, d. 1837) gives almost the exact case discussed here in answer to a question asked of him by Abraham Oppenheimer. The woman was eight months pregnant when she died. A skilled doctor said that she is definitely dead, and that the baby is alive. Accepting the opinion of the skilled physician, both doubts mentioned above are canceled. The woman is definitely dead, so the doubt mentioned by Isserles that we have not the skill to be sure when a person is dead is now obviated; and the physician says that the child is definitely alive, so the doubt discussed by Rashi and the Talmud that we may be violating the Sabbath (if this occurred on the Sabbath) for an unnecessary purpose (since the child may be dead) is also obviated. Therefore, Moses Kunitz said that the physician should operate and does not even need to ask permission of the Jewish ecclesiastical court. Moses Kunitz here actually uses the word "Caesarean," and gives the origin of the term (namely, that Julius Caesar was born by such an operation).

Jacob Reischer, Rabbi of Metz two centuries ago, in his Responsa *(Shevut Yaakov* 1.13, at the end), not only gives permission for such an operation but ends his responsum by saying that he who performs it must be praised for doing so and his reward will be great. See also Abraham of Buczacz (*Eshel Avraham* to *Orah Hayim* 330), who cites an authority who praises the physician for prompt action to save the child.

There is, of course, a possible complication somewhat related to this question. Since the child will die unless the operation is performed very quickly, I was asked a number of years ago by a physician whether - if the mother is not quite dead, but is definitely dying (for example, of cancer) - we may not make sure to save the child by performing the operation before the mother is dead, although it is certain that the operation itself will definitely put an end to the mother's life. See the discussion of this special question in *Reform Responsa*, pp. 214ff.

But this is a special form of the question and does not apply directly here, where the physician assures us that the mother is dead. See further discussion of the matter in Eliezer Spiro (*Der Muncaczer*) in his *Minhat Eliezer* IV.28, and Greenwald in *Kol Bo Al Avelut*, p. 49, section 18, and pp. 43ff.

To sum up: if it is certain that the mother is dead and that the child is alive, there is no question that the Caesarean operation not only may be performed, but must be performed, and is indeed deemed praiseworthy.

*Walter Jacob, *American Reform Responsa* ed., New York 1983, #80

LIVING WILL

Walter Jacob

QUESTION: What is the Jewish attitude toward a "living will"? (Loren Roseman, Norcross GA)*

ANSWER: The "living will" provides a legal method in some thirty-seven states for terminating life support systems in the case of individuals who are dying because of serious illness or accident. The pain of family members or friends in comas over long periods of time and in a "persistent vegetative state" while attached to life preserving machinery has led to the consideration of such documents. At that juncture often no one will agree on what should be done. In some occasions the courts have intervened; in others eventually a family member or physician intervenes, but at the risk of subsequent legal action.

Those who wish to spare their family from this agonizing decision may decide on a "living will", a form frequently used with a proxy designation statement reads as follows:

Living Will Declaration

To My Family, Physician
and Medical Facility
I,.........., being of sound mind, voluntarily make known my desire that my dying shall not be artificially prolonged under the following circumstances:

If I should have an injury, disease or illness regarded by my physician as incurable and terminal, and if my physician determines that the application of life-sustaining procedures would serve only to prolong artificially the dying process, I direct that such procedures be withheld or withdrawn and that I be permitted to die. I want treatment limited to those measures that will provide me with maximum comfort and freedom from pain. Should I become unable to participate in decisions with respect to my medical treatment, it is my intention that these directions be honored by my family and physicians(s) as a final expression of my legal right to refuse medical treatment, and I accept the consequences of this refusal.

Signed.................................Date.........................Witness.....
....
............Witness.........................

Designation Clause (optional*)

Should I become comatose, incompetent or otherwise mentally or physically incapable of communication, I
authorize..............................
presently residing at...
to make treatment decisions on my behalf in accordance with my Living Will Declaration and my understanding of Judaism. I have discussed my wishes concerning terminal care with this person, and I trust his/her judgment on my behalf.

Signed.........................Date......................
Witness....................Witness....................

*If I have not designated a proxy as provided above, I understand that my Living Will Declaration shall nevertheless be given effect should the appropriate circumstances arise.

The various statutes specifically exclude chronic debilitating diseases such as Alzheimers which are not life threatening and attempt to deal with other problems as well.

This approach raises many questions about traditional and modern Jewish perceptions of life and death. Is this akin to suicide or euthanasia? Suicide has always been considered a major sin (*A. Z.* 18a; *Semahot* 2.2; *Shulhan Arukh Yoreh Deah* 345.2) and even its contemplation was considered wrong. We have also felt that euthanasia is not consistent with our tradition (W. Jacob ed., *American Reform Responsa* #78, 79). We may see from the arguments presented in these two responsa that nothing positive may be done to encourage death, however, the "Living Will" is not euthanasia, but an instrument of antidysthanonic. Our tradition has felt that a *goses* (dying person) should also not be kept from dying after all hope for recovery has passed, and so the *Sefer Hassidim* stated that if the steady rhythm of someone chopping wood kept a *goses* alive, the wood chopping should be stopped (#723; Isserles to *Shulhan Arukh Yoreh Deah* 339.1). Some rabbinic statements limit the definition of *goses* to persons who will not live for more than three days, however modern medical technology has made these limitations obsolete. Earlier Biblical statements clearly indicated that no positive acts to abbreviate life, even, when there was no hope, were permitted (I Sam 31.1 ff; II Sam 1.5 ff). In a later age Solomon Eger indicated that medicine should also not be used to hinder a soul's departure (comment to *Shulhan Arukh Yoreh Deah* 339.1). We may then safely say that at the critical juncture of life when no hope for recovery exists the soul should be allowed to drift away peacefully. We have become even more sensitive to issues of euthanasia through our own experiences with the Holocaust.

Love of life in all its forms is very much part of our tradition. Even when conditions of life are rather doubtful and when there might be serious questions about the "quality of life" we cannot encourage euthanasia (W. Jacob *Contemporary American Reform Responsa* #83) nor can we make assumptions about "the quality of life."

The modern development of medicine has brought wonderful cures and provides additional years of life even to those in advanced years. On the other hand its technology may leave us in a permanent coma or a persistent vegetative state in which we are neither alive nor dead. Such individuals may be completely dependent upon life support machinery. While this is acceptable during periods of recovery, we fear a permanent coma when the mind has ceased to respond and a plateau of mere physical existence has been reached.

When the Harvard criteria of death have been satisfied, life support machinery may be removed. This state of "brain dead" has been defined by an ad hoc committee of the Harvard Medical School in 1968 *(Journal of the American Medical Association* Vol 205, pp 337 ff). It recommended three tests: (1) Lack of response to external stimuli or to internal need; (2) absence of movement and breathing as observed by physicians over a period of at least one hour; (3) absence of elicitable reflexes; and a fourth criterion to confirm the other three; (4) a flat or isoelectric electroencephalogram. The group also suggested that this examination be repeated after an interval of twenty-four hours. Several Orthodox authorities have accepted these criteria while others have rejected them. Moses Feinstein felt that they could be accepted along with shutting off the respirator briefly in order to see whether independent breathing was continuing *(Igrot Mosheh Yoreh Deah* #174). Moses Tendler has gone somewhat further and has accepted the Harvard criteria *(Journal of American Medical Association* Vol 238 #15 pp 165 ff). David Bleich *(Hapardes, Tevet* 5737) and Jacob Levy *(Hadarom Nisan* 5731 *Tishri* 5730; *Noam* 5.30) have vigorously rejected these criteria as they feel that life must have ceased entirely with the heart no longer functioning, a condition belatedly established by Hatam Sofer in the eighteenth century *(Responsa Hatam Sofer Yoreh Deah* #338). We can see that although the question has not been resolved by our Orthodox colleagues, some of them have certainly accepted the recommendations of the Harvard Medical School committee. We are satisfied that these criteria comply with our concern that life has ended. Therefore, when circulation and respiration only continue through mechanical means, as established by the above-mentioned tests, then the suffering of the patient and his/her family may be permitted to cease, as no "natural independent life" functions have been sustained. We would permit a physician in good conscience to cease treatment and to remove life giving support systems. The "persistent vegetative state" is more difficult as "brain death" has not yet been reached. Such an individual would be considered a *goses* who is considered to be a living human being in all respects *(Semahot* 1.1; *Yad Hil. Evel* 4.5; *Tur* and *Shulhan Arukh Yoreh Deah* 339.1 ff.). One may desecrate the Sabbath to help him according to Jacob Reischer *(Shevut Yaakov* 1:13), though others *(Kenesset Hagadol)* disagreed.

The long discussions about a *goses* indicate that no positive actions to hasten death may be taken, so he/she is not to be moved or his/her eyes closed, etc. As stated above there is no prohibition against diminishing pain or increasing the person's comfort or initiating new treatment which will not change the condition of the patient. Under these circumstances a "Living Will" may be helpful although we realize that we know little of the "inner life" of people in this state; we do not wish to terminate what may still be significant to them.

It would be permissible according to this point of view to help and assist those who may need to make these kinds of judgments for us in the future through a "Living Will". This may be especially important if there is no one present who can be counted on to make an appropriate decision in keeping with our verbally expressed wishes. The document must be worded so that it deals with the "persistent vegetative state" without moving toward euthanasia. The document should be sufficiently recent to assure that it reflects the wishes of the patient.

All of us wish for a reasonable exit from this world and would also like to make that period as bearable as possible for ourselves and our surviving family. The positive outlook on life which governs Judaism prohibits any drastic steps toward death but it does not insist that life continue when the person is a *goses*. At that point a peaceful release is permitted. The "Living Will" provides one possibility; the appointment of a proxy provides another.

March 1989

*Walter Jacob, *Questions and Reform Jewish Answers - New American Reform Responsa*, New York, 1992, #156.

CHOOSING WHICH PATIENT TO SAVE

Solomon B. Freehof

QUESTION: The head of a clinic in Boston asked, following a forum session at the last Biennial Convention of the Union of American Hebrew Congregations in Montreal (November, 1967): "What guidance can Jewish tradition give us in the excruciating, ethical dilemma of selecting one patient over many others to keep him alive by means of a mechanical kidney machine? Since such facilities are extremely limited, many patients must be rejected and are certain to die. The same question may also be raised with reference to the very limited supply of organs for transplantation. On what basis can a conscientious doctor make the decision as to which patient is to live or die?"*

ANSWER: Solomon Landau, in a responsum embodied in the collection of his father Ezekiel Landau's responsa (*Noda biYehudah*, vol. II, #74), was asked whether a man sought by the government as a criminal should be turned over or not. He says at the outset: "It is difficult to make a decision in matters which involve the life of a human being." Such a decision is always a difficult one in any decent tradition, religious or social. The question asked here by the physician of the clinic is especially difficult to decide on the basis of Jewish traditional literature. Obviously, there were in those days no such remarkable inventions, or the means for the preservation of vital organs, as there are today. In those days, when a person was dying, they would discourage any artificial attempt to keep him alive for another hour or so, because a man has a right to die when the time comes (cf. *Ran* to *Nedarim* 40a). But nowadays it is possible, in the case of moribund patients, to effect what often amounts to a cure. So there is no real precedent for the problem in the traditional literature.

Nevertheless, there are quite a number of somewhat different discussions which involve the question of choosing one person to live or another person to die. In the discussion of these various dilemmas there may perhaps be found an ethical principle, or at least an ethical mood, which might help indicate what Jewish *tradition would have said* in a situation such as this one which now occurs frequently in modern hospitals.

The *Mishnah* (*Oholot* VII.6) deals with a question which involves the choosing between one life and another. A mother is apparently dying because of the childbirth. Either she or her child can be saved. Which one should it be? The law is that the child is looked upon as an assailant and therefore may be destroyed before he kills the mother. Therefore, the unborn child should be destroyed, and the mother saved. If, however, the child puts forth its head, then it may no longer be destroyed. It is now considered a separate person, and now the law is thus stated: "We do not dispose of [or push aside] one person in favor of another" (cf. also *Sanhedrin* 72b). This is stated as the fixed law in the *Shulhan Arukh, Hoshen Mishpat* 425.2).

This clear-cut principle that we may not save one life at the expense of another seemed at first glance to be somewhat contradicted by the discussion in the Mishnah and the Talmud as to the relative respect to be paid to a father and to a teacher. This *Mishnah* (*Baba Metzia* II. 11) says that if a person finds an object lost by his father and another object lost by his teacher, he must first return the one lost by his teacher. The Mishnah explains the reasons as follows: "For his father has brought him into the light of this world, while his teacher, who teaches him wisdom, has brought him into the light of the world to come." Upon that basis the Mishnah continues to say that if both his father and his teacher are held in captivity, he must first redeem his teacher and after that redeem his father. This is discussed in the Talmud in *Baba Metzia* 33a, and is codified as law by Maimonides in *Yad Hil. Avodah* 12.2 and in the *Shulhan Arukh, Yoreh Deah* 242.34. All this seems to contradict the principle that you may not choose one life to save in preference to another, but actually this is not so. The Rabbis do not speak here of such an irreversible fact as death, but only at most of captivity in which both are to be saved (except, of course, that they give the order as to who should be saved first). When it comes to an actual matter of life or death, in which a choice is final, the principle remains that one life is as precious as another. This principle that we do not destroy one life in order to save another is further exemplified in a discussion in *Pesahim* 25b. A man comes before Rava and says: "The governor of my city has given me the alternative that either I should kill so-and-so or the governor will kill me. What shall I do? Rava answered him: "Be killed rather than kill. What makes you think that your blood is redder than his?"

This Talmudic phrase, "Your blood is redder than his," was used in rather a reverse sense in the latest volume of Eliezer Waldenberg, *Tzitz Eliezer*, vol. 9, 45, Jerusalem, 1967. In this volume, devoted to a large extent to modern medical questions, the author concludes that a person is certainly not *required* by law to donate an organ of his body in order that it may be planted into the body of another. If he is endangered by the removal of the organ, then he is actually forbidden to risk his life. Of course, if the danger to him were minimal and the benefit to the recipient were maximal, it would be a good deed; but, otherwise, one should not endanger his life in this way because one life - in this case his own - is as valuable as the life he wishes to save. Waldenberg then uses the Talmudic dictum cited above: "What makes you think (that his blood is redder than yours)?" But whichever way the phrase is taken, its meaning is clear enough: Every life is as equally valuable as any other life.

The two instances - that of the infant and that of the man ordered to become a murderer - both differ from the case inquired about here because these two cases involve actually taking steps to put people to death, while the case of the clinic involves merely allowing dying people to die. Nevertheless, in spite of this difference, this much at least is relevant: we have no right to say that one person's life is more important than that of the other - the mother's or the child's, or the man's or his intended victim's. From the standpoint of religion, all people are alike in status as to the right to life.

There is still another set of circumstances developed in a series of discussions in the literature, all of which spring from the same Biblical account. These discussions, different from those above, do not deal with the worth of one person rather than another, but with the safety of a social group as against the life of one person. The question now is whether a city or a group may save itself by handing over one of its number to death. In the Second Book of Samuel, chapter 20, Sheva ben Bichri, who rebelled against King David, takes refuge in the city of Abel. There he is pursued by Joab and his army, which surrounds the city and threatens to destroy it. The wise woman of the city gives up Sheva to Joab, and thus the city is spared. This incident is discussed in the *Tosefta (Terumot*, end of chapter 7) and in the Palestinian Talmud (*Terumot*, end of chapter 8), where it is cited as a guide in the following situation. A group of travelers is stopped by brigands who say to the travelers: "Give us one of your number. We will kill him and let the rest of you go." May they do so? This, now, is a case of saving a large number of people by having one person die. The decision is that they must say: "No, we would rather all be killed than give up one of our number to death" (since the shedding of blood is one of the three sins for which a person must be willing to die rather than commit it, the other two being idolatry and immorality). The conclusion is, so far, that rather than commit what amounts to one murder, we would rather be killed ourselves, even though there are twenty of us and the victim would be only one.

However, the discussion in the *Tosefta* and in the Talmud continues as follows: This wholesale self-sacrifice applies only when the brigands are not specific and merely say "one of you," thus compelling us to choose the man to be killed. But if they are specific and they are searching for a certain man whom they mention by name, then we do not all have to be killed for his sake, since it is not we who selected him for death. This, however, is only one opinion. The opposite opinion is that this one man, even though specifically named, may not be turned over to the brigands unless he is criminal, as Sheva was in the Biblical account, since he rebelled against King David. This distinction is embodied in the law (Maimonides, *Yad Hilhot Yesodei Torah* V.5). There is some disagreement about whether the man needs to be a known criminal before he is surrendered to save the lives of all the others, or whether it is sufficient if the brigands named him and it is not we who have selected him. See the discussion by Joseph Karo in *Kesef Mishneh* to the law in Maimonides.

The bearing of this discussion on the case in point is that actually the other patients, who will not be given the rare remedy, have not been directly selected for death. They have already been marked for death by forces beyond the physician's control (as by the brigands in this case), and if they die, it is not directly the physician's fault. They would die anyhow. It is not he who has really named them for death.

It is also clear from this aversion against turning someone over to death in order to save someone else, or even a group, that it would be absolutely forbidden by the spirit of Jewish law to hasten the death of some terminal patient already marked for death in order to take something from his body in order to save another patient or for the increase of medical knowledge.

But so far all of the incidents cited involve a direct choice betwee·- living and healthy people as to who should live and who should die. The case involved in the question asked is of people who are dying. Is there any guidance in the law for choosing between people who are already marked for death? It is possible to say that, since they are already dying, we should just let them all die and not attempt the bitter choice of picking one of them to live. Is such a "hands-off" attitude permissible?

This very question, by close analogy, is discussed in the Talmud (*Baba Metzia*, 62a). The case is stated as follows: Two men are walking (presumably in the desert). They have one pitcher of water which contains enough to keep only one of them alive long enough to cross the desert safely. If both of them drink, they will both die. If one drinks, he

151

will be saved and the other will die. What shall be done? Ben Petura said: "Let them both die and let not one be a witness to the death of his fellow man." But Rabbi Akiva's greater authority is cited to refute this opinion of Ben Petura. He says: "Your life comes first." In other words, a man must strive to save his own life. Although this narrative is cited in a discussion about the taking of interest and whether it should be returned, nevertheless it constitutes an independent homily (see the statement of Asher ben Yehiel to the passage). While, of course, Akiva's decision is not directly helpful to the question of deciding which shall live (since it does not indicate in which manner the matter will be settled with each one trying to save his own life); nevertheless, this much is clear: We may not permit both men to die when at least one of them can be saved. The passage is unfortunately too terse, and therefore we cannot tell the method of selection, but it is clear enough that a selection will and should be made, and that it is not right to allow both of them to die merely because it would be painful to make a decision. Thus, the final problem still remains. He should choose, but which one?

As to whom he chooses, there is, in a sense, a negative guideline. The passage which speaks of the brigands or captors demanding one of the group of men to be given up for death, speaks first of a group of captive women. The captors ask for one woman to be given to them for sexual abuse. The sexual fate of a captive woman receives considerable discussion in the law. The married status of the captive wife may be affected by what had happened to her during her captivity. If one of the women in the group has already been abused, the other women may not say that since this unfortunate one has already been abused, she is the one who should be given up. (*See Kesef Mishneh to Yad Hil. Yesodei Torah*, V. 5, where Caro cites the responsa of Solomon b. Aderet to this effect.) They have no right to decide on the basis of her unhappy past and so select her in order to save themselves.

In other words, in matters which are equivalent to life or death (as this was considered to be), the past status or character of the prospective victim may not be considered. We may not say: "This one's

152

life may be set aside in favor of the other's." All are of equal status in relation to life or death.

There is, however, some other standard of choice before the physician, one which is precisely relevant. There is a discussion in the Talmud (*Avoda Zarah* 27b) which is developed in the legal literature into a principle. It can be stated as follows: [When there is a chance for a cure] we do not put too much value upon the last hours of a dying man (*Ein mashgihim lechayei sha-ah*). In other words, these last few hours are not so valuable that we may not risk them if we want to try out some new and hitherto untried remedy. These last hours are fading anyhow. So Jacob Reischer, Rabbi of Metz (died 1733), in his responsa (*Shevut Yaakov* III, #75) concludes that we may risk the few hours of a dying man and try an untried remedy, if there is a fair prospect that he can be cured enough to have, say, a year of life. He says at first that even the *hayei shaah* (the remaining hours of life) are important and we must guard them (i.e., we never *hasten* death); nevertheless, if there is a remedy by use of which it is possible to cure him, then in that case we may risk it. The same decision was arrived at in a responsum published this past year by Mordecai Jacob Breisch (*Helkat Yaakov* III, #141). From this we conclude that the physician must endeavor to decide not on the basis of personality reasons, but on medical grounds. He must select the patient - rich or poor, good or bad - who has the better prospect of survival and of getting more of a relatively healthy life. As for the others, no direct action should be taken by him against them. Their sickness will run its course.

This same conclusion, i.e., that the one who will benefit most should receive the remedy, was arrived at over a hundred and fifty years ago by Joseph Teomim (1727-1793). Of course, he could not have had any knowledge of modern transplants, nor of the special problems involved in them. He came to his conclusion purely on the basis of the spirit of the law. His statement is in his commentary *Peri Megadim* to *Shulhan Arukh, Orah Hayim* 328 (commenting on the *Magen David*). The *Shulhan Arukh* at that point deals with the question of which patients

153

may have the Sabbath violated for them and to what extent. The discussion involves the question of which patient is in real danger and which is not in immediate danger. Joseph Teomim then widens his conclusion from the Sabbath law to a more general application and says: If there is doubt about whether one patient is in danger, and there is no doubt that the other patient is in danger - if there is not enough medicine for both of them, we give it to the one who is in greater danger.

From all this discussion in the Talmudic and later literature, a certain mood emerges. First, that one life is as important as another; and this must certainly be so in the eyes of the physician. Second, that actively to take steps to destroy another life for our own benefit is not permitted. Third, that when it comes to a choice between people who are dying anyway, the choice cannot be evaded, but must be made (nothing is gained by allowing both men to die in the desert!). But as to whom to choose for survival, it must be on purely medical grounds, selecting the one who has a better chance of benefiting from the remedy. Of course, this is not an absolute test, because out of ten patients there may be two or three who could greatly benefit from the remedy. But at least this principle narrows the choice and in many cases can decide the case. So, while there is no case in Jewish legal tradition precisely like this modern question, there is enough in it to give at least this much guidance.

Addendum:

Dr. Julius Kravetz, a member of our committee, calls my attention to a sequence of passages in Mishnah and Talmud which points in the opposite direction from the conclusion arrived at above. These passages should be mentioned, not only for the sake of completeness, but also as a possible balance to the opinion expressed in the responsum.

The *Mishnah (Horayot* III.7,8) says that a man precedes a woman (i.e., has prior right) "to be kept alive" (*lehahayot*) and to have his lost articles returned. But a woman precedes a man in being provided with clothing and being redeemed from captivity. A Cohen has precedence over a Levi, a Levi over an Israelite, and an Israelite over an illegitimate, etc.

The Talmud discusses this Mishnah in two places: *Horayot* 13bff and *Nazir* 47b. In both passages the Talmud gives the reasons for the various priorities. There is, however, a further development in the passage in *Nazir*. Mar Ukba says that the priority (of the Battlepriest over the *Segan*) means that he has precedence in our duty to keep him alive. The *Tosafot* are still more specific, saying that if a heap has fallen on both, it is he who must be rescued first. Rabbi Untermann (*HaTorah Vehamedinah* IV, 22-29) takes this as the meaning of the discussion in the Mishnah and applies it in the case of a pharmacist having a limited supply of penicillin, etc.

This, then, is a *halakhic* discussion which points to an order of precedence in the saving of lives (a man before a woman, a Priest before a Levite, etc.). However, it seems to me that the discussion, in spite of the *Tosafot*, does not necessarily refer to the rescue of endangered lives. The Mishna uses the word *lehahayot*. If the Mishnah meant "to rescue from danger," we would have expected it to use the word *lehatzil*. In fact, the *Shach* (*Yoreh Deah* 351.14) says that the word does mean *lehatzil* and interprets accordingly. But the Mishnah uses this word in precisely the same way in which it is used in Psalm 33:19. The Psalm makes use of both words, *lehatzil* and *lehahayot*, each for a specific thought. It says "to rescue (*lehatzil*) thee from death, and to sustain thee (*lehahayot*) in famine." So our Mishnah here uses the word *lehahayot* precisely in connection with providing clothing and ransoming from captivity. If our Mishnah had actually meant "to rescue from death," then we would expect that the codifiers, when giving the laws of rescue, would refer to this priority. But neither Maimonides, nor the *Tur*, nor the *Shulhan Arukh* mention any of these priorities in the laws of rescue (cf. *Yad, Hilchot Rotzeach* I 14; *Tur* and *Shulhan Arukh, Hoshen Mishpat* 42b).

155

Judging by the context of this Mishnah and by the Biblical use of the word in the Psalm, *lehahayot* is not used here loosely as meaning the same as *lehatzil*, but precisely as meaning "to keep alive," in the sense of "to sustain or to support."

This is clearly the way in which the codifiers understood the discussion. They do mention the list of personal priorities, but only in connection with charity. So Maimonides (*Yad Hil. Matnat Aniyim* VIII.15-17), the *Tur* and *Shulhan Arukh* (*Yoreh Deah* 251).

*Walter Jacob, *American Reform Responsa* ed., New York, 1983, #75.

A MEDICAL EXPERIMENT

Walter Jacob

QUESTION: A patient is afflicted with a fatal disease which leads to an unpleasant death. An effort to control it for a short period of time (less than one year) can be made through using drugs which in the final stages have the following side effects: The body skin peels constantly and this is accompanied by pain which no drug will alleviate. Some researchers feel that the full effects of the medicine can only be studied through such human utilization. Should a physician permit his patient to undergo this treatment? (Rabbi Mark Staitman, Pittsburgh PA)*

ANSWER: The general principles governing our question are fully discussed by the modern Israeli authority, A. Abraham (*Lev Avraham* Vol II pp 75-76; Meiri to *San.* 84b; I.Y. Unterman *Noam* Vol 12 pp 5 ff). He stated that no doctor has the right to subject another person to a medical experiment even though such an experiment may eventually help others. The doctor may expose himself/herself to danger (*safeq sakana*) when she/he attends an infectious patient, as that is her/his duty as a physician, but he cannot ask a patient to submit to danger. The author adds that if the experiment is *not* dangerous, then the patient may participate in it and that would be reckoned as a *mitzvah*. Eliezer Waldenberg (*Tzitz Eliezer* Vol XIII #103; Moses Sofer *Hatam Sofer Yoreh Deah* #76) disagreed with this view of safe experiments and denied any religious obligation even when there was no danger. At the most, one may permit such participation, but it is in no sense a religious duty (*mitzvah*).

It is a general rule that every person should avoid danger to life. So, the *Talmud* (*Ber.* 3a; *Shab.* 32a) warned people against walking among ruined buildings as a weak wall may collapse. The Talmud (*Hul.* 10a) stated that danger to life and health was of greater concern than religious prohibitions (*hamira saqanta meissura*). In other words, one must exercise greater care to avoid danger than a religious prohibition.

This general rule of avoiding danger is, however, confronted with the duty of rescuing a fellow human. Discussion of these issues have continued through the centuries (Lev.19.16; *San.* 73a; *Yad Hil Rotzeah Ushemirat Nefesh* 1:2, 14, 15; *Shulhan Arukh Hoshen Mishpat* 426). The question then is to what extent we may endanger ourselves in order to help others. There is no doubt that we must assist our fellow human beings, but where are the limits? This question has been discussed in a rather picturesque responsa of the 16th century scholar David ibn Zimri of Egypt (Vol III #627): The Pasha told a certain Jew to allow his leg to be amputated or else he (the Pasha) would kill another Jew. May this man endanger his life through the amputation in order to save the life of a fellow Jew? David ibn Zimri considered this beyond the call of duty.

The medieval *Sefer Hassidim* (#467 ed. Margolis) described a medicine which cured or killed the patient in nine days. The book prohibited the drug on the basis that it might kill the patient before his time *(qodem zemano)*. A number of later authorities have agreed with this assessment *(Shevut Yaaqov* I #13, III #85; *Binyan Zion* #111; *Hatam Sofer Yoreh Deah* #76).

In this instance the patient appears to be doomed by the disease, and both patient and doctor have a choice whether to use this experimental treatment which leads to a horrifying death or whether a natural death somewhat sooner and also unpleasant shall be permitted. No one should persuade the patient to undertake this therapy which leads to a terrible death even if the patient may wish to help others and to use the last portion of his/her life in some useful fashion. In this instance the weeks of agony before death are so terrible that we can not justify the "treatment". It is unlikely that the patient or the family will be able to imagine the horrifying nature of this death. We should therefore do everything possible to persuade the attending physician not to suggest this treatment. If he/she feels that it must be mentioned then to put it into the bleakest possible context so that the patient is unlikely to choose it.

We cannot justify an experiment which will cause long terrible suffering through the vague hope that it will eventually produce a cure for others. The researchers who are working on this project must devise another means of testing their therapy.

February 1991

*Walter Jacob, *Questions and Reform Jewish Answers, New American Reform Responsa*, New York, 1992, # 152.

A DANGEROUS MEDICAL EXPERIMENT

Walter Jacob

QUESTION: A man with a severe heart disease and no more than six months to live wants to know whether he may participate in a controlled experiment with a new drug; he is anxious to do so. Since the purpose of the experiment is to save lives in the future, may he participate even though there is some danger of shortening his life-span? His own chance for a cure at this late stage of the disease is slight. (H. T., Los Angeles, CA)*

ANSWER: It is a general rule that every person should avoid danger to life. So, the *Talmud* (*Berakhot* 3a; *Shabbat* 32a) said that a person should not walk among ruined buildings because of the danger that a shaky wall may collapse. The *Talmud* (*Hulin* 10a) stated that danger to life and health was of greater concern than religious prohibitions (*hamira saqanta tamira*). In other words, one must exercise greater care to avoid danger than a religious prohibition.

The general rule of guarding against danger is, however, confronted by the duty of rescuing a fellow human from danger. This has been discussed from early times by our tradition (Lev. 19.16; *Sanhedrin* 73a; *Shulhan Arukh Hoshen Mishpat* 426). The question then is whether we may endanger ourselves in order to help others. There is no doubt that we must assist our fellowman through our means or influence, but are we permitted or required to go further? This question has been discussed in a rather picturesque way by David Ibn Zimri of Egypt (16th century). In his responsa (Vol. III, #627), the following incident was cited: The Pasha told a certain Jew to allow his leg to be amputated or else he (the Pasha) would kill another Jew. May this man endanger his life (since the amputation was dangerous) in order to save the life of a fellow Jew? David Ibn Zimri considered this beyond the call of duty.

The medieval *Sefer Hassidim* (#467, ed., Margolis) described a medicine which cured or killed the patient in nine days. The book prohibited the drug on the basis that it might kill the patient before his time (*qodem zemano*). A number of later authorities have agreed with this assessment *(Shevut Yaaqov,* Vol. I, #13, Vol. 3, #75; *Binyan Zion,* #111, *Hatam Sofer Yoreh Deah #76).*

The general principles governing our question are fully discussed by the modern Israeli authority, A. Abraham *(Lev Avraham,* Vol. II, pp. 75-76). He states that no doctor has the right to subject another person to a medical experiment even though such an experiment may eventually help others. The doctor may expose himself to danger *(safeq sakana)* when he attends an infectious patient, as that is his duty as a physician, but he cannot ask a patient to submit to a dangerous experiment. The author adds that if the experiment is *not* dangerous, then the patient may participate in it and that would be reckoned as a *mitzvah.* Eliezer Waldenberg *(Tzitz Eliezer,* Vol. XIII, #103) disagrees with this view of safe experiments and denies any religious obligation even when there is no danger. At the most, one may permit such participation, but it is in no sense a religious duty *(mitzvah).*

We would generally agree with the tradition and the decision reached by Dr. Abraham, yet our patient's desire to participate must also be considered. The need and *mitzvah* to help others through his part in such experiments is important. Tradition would reject any participation, but we may argue that as we have benefited from medical progress, we must help to continue it.

We must ask many questions before we reach a decision. Is the patient fully informed? Does he have the capacity to understand the implications of his choice? Has this been discussed by him with his family? What actually is the risk benefit ratio?

We would permit participation in an experiment of limited risk and doubtful benefit by this patient if these questions have been answered and if he is certain that this would give meaning and purpose to the last phase of his life. Many individuals search for some useful act during this period, and the experiment may provide it for this individual and his family. If successful, it may, of course, also prolong his life somewhat.

August 1985

*Walter Jacob, *Contemporary American Reform Responsa*, New York, 1987, # 17

NUTRITION AND INCURABLE CANCER

Walter Jacob

QUESTION: Should nutrition in contrast to medicine be continued for a comatose patient who is suffering from incurable cancer? (Stanley Landman, San Antonio TX)*

ANSWER: We need to make some distinctions immediately between a terminal cancer patient and a victim of stroke or an accident. In the latter cases, the prognosis is not at all certain and death may not be indicated in the foreseeable future. In the case of the incurable cancer patient, a time is reached when medicine can no longer be considered as healing and when the suffering patient is being kept alive artificially with no potential of improvement. When we have reached this point and nothing more can be done, then we may justifiably state that we are dealing with a *goses* and should remove obstacles which may lead to an easier death (*Ket.* 104a; *Ned.* 40a; *Sefer Hassidim* #723; Isserles to *Shulhan Arukh Yoreh Deah* 339.1; *Even Haezer* 121.7; *Hoshen Mishpat* 221.2 and commentaries). We are willing to utilize modern medical criteria determine when this stage has been reached (W. Jacob ed., *American Reform Responsa* #79 etc). We realize that these criteria will be refined as medicine is making rapid strides. Medical and technical means need not be continued when the patient is dying and is only being kept alive through these means.

Now let us look at nutrition specifically. We should not think of it in terms of the meals which we normally eat but rather of nutrition provided intravenously or through a stomach tube. Both of these methods are certainly appropriate when they are part of the healing process and help the patient toward a cure. They should, however, be discontinued, just as medication when only they and medicine are artificially keeping the patient who is dying (*goses*) alive. Such feeding does not help the patient and at best must be debilitating and uncomfortable, if not painful. We should also realize that diminished interest by those patients normally capable of eating is another sign that life is ebbing and that the last stages have been reached. Our main goal should be the patient's comfort.

Nutrition artificially introduced at the last stage of life should be seen as a hinderance to death and may be stopped, along with medication. At the appropriate time, the family should be able, in clear conscience, in line with Jewish tradition, to make this decision together with their physician.

August 1991

*Walter Jacob, *Questions and Reform Jewish Answers, New American Reform Responsa,* New York, 1992, #159

DRUGS TO RELIEVE PAIN

Walter Jacob

QUESTION: Does Jewish tradition set a limit to the use of drugs in order to alleviate pain? Frequently, physicians seem hesitant to prescribe drugs due to the fear of addiction or other reasons. What is our attitude toward pain and its alleviation? (Rena T. Hirsh, Santa Barbara CA)*

ANSWER: Jewish tradition is not ascetic and does not endorse self affliction through pain. The only exception is *Yom Kippur,* along with some of the lesser fast days. On that day we are commanded to "afflict our souls," but that does not entail real suffering, only fasting and abstinence from sexual intercourse. Even fasting is not necessary for those who are physically impaired. We feel no necessity to renounce this world and its blessings and so need not afflict ourselves in order to attain salvation in the next world. This is in vivid contrast to some forms of Christianity.

It is true that rabbinic tradition has interpreted the suffering of the people of Israel and of individuals, as either Divine punishment or as a test (Job; *B. B.* 5a; *Shabbat* 55a, etc). However, none of these sources and many others, has anyone been asked to seek suffering, rather than try to avoid it. During illness we may use every medical means available to avoid pain *(Shulhan Arukh Yoreh Deah* 241.13 and commentaries).

There are enormous variations in the pain threshold of individuals. Many physicians refuse to consider this or do not appropriately deal with the entire issue of pain. Sometimes this is because specialists, who do not communicate with each other, are treating the patient; each is concerned with a specific organ or system and none is aware of the total effect on the patient. At other times, it is simply due to indifference and a lack of interest in the patient, possibly because the attending physician has never suffered any serious pain. There is certainly nothing within Jewish tradition which would restrain the treatment of pain. We would have a greater fear of continuous pain than addiction.

We must be equally concerned with pain of the terminally ill. There is a fine line of distinction between alleviating pain and prescribing a drug which may hasten death. When the pain is great the physician should alleviate the pain and not be overly concerned about the latter consequence, as death is certain in any case. (W. Jacob ed., *American Reform Responsa* #79, etc).

There is nothing within Jewish tradition that would keep pain relieving drugs from being given when medically indicated. We would hope that the patient be made as comfortable as possible and that this will help recovery or make the last days of life easier.

August 1991

*Walter Jacob, *Questions and Reform Jewish Answers - New American Reform Responsa*, New York, 1992, #151.

AN ELDERLY PATIENT WHO REFUSES DIALYSIS

Walter Jacob

QUESTION: An intelligent, articulate, eighty-three year old widow has renal disease which can be treated by kidney dialysis. She was diagnosed eight years ago and refused dialysis. Since then her health has generally deteriorated with a hip fracture, incontinence and heart disease. She has now entered a nursing home and suffers from end-stage renal disease as well as congestive heart failure. She has made it clear to her brother, as well as those at the nursing home, that she wishes no drastic treatments (CPR, mechanical ventilation, feeding tubes, etc.) but wants to die *peacefully and without pain.* One of the attending physicians feels a strong obligation to save this patient's life. He argues that he cannot let her die of renal kidney disease and wants to impose dialysis upon her. Should she be forced to undergo dialysis? What are her rights and obligations and what are those of the physician in this case? (Rabbi Dayle Friedman, Philadelphia PA)

ANSWER: A good deal has been written about the obligations of a physician to heal. Our tradition from *Talmudic* times onward has encouraged the use of every possible medical procedure in order to save lives. The discussions were based on "He shall cause him to be thoroughly healed" (Ex 21.20) and "You shall not stand idly by the blood of your fellow" (Lev 19.16). Even risky procedures may be undertaken if the physician thinks that there is a reasonable hope for recovery (San 73a; A Z b; J. Reischer *Shevut Yaakov* III #85; Eliezer Waldenberg, *Tzitz Eliezer* 10 #25 Chap 5 Sec 5; Moshe Feinstein *Igrot Moshe*h Yoreh Deah 2 #59; I. Y. Unterman *Noam* 12 p 5; W. Jacob (ed) *American Reform Responsa* #75, 76, 77, 79; W. Jacob *Contemporary American Reform Responsa* #77, 85). We have gone somewhat further and permitted a patient who understands the risks, to be part of a dangerous medical experiment in which the chances of recovery are slim (W. Jacob *Contemporary American Reform Responsa* #17).

Patients have always been encouraged to use physicians and to follow the Biblical dictum "Heal yourself". Physicians have been held in high regard from early times onward *(Ben Sirah* 38.1; *Tobit* 2.10,

Midrash Rabbah Exodus 21.7; see also I. Jakobovits *Jewish Medical Ethics* pp 201 ff). On the other hand skepticism about physicians has also played its role in Jewish life; the *Mishnah* quotes R. Judah: "The best among physicians is destined for hell", *(M* Kid 4.14). All of these sources establish the physicians duty to heal as well as the patient's obligation to maintain good health and to do whatever is considered reasonable to regain health.

It has been established that nothing positive may be done to hasten death even in a terminal patient, yet, there is also no obligation to intervene in a hopeless situation to minimally prolong life (S. B. Freehof *Modern Reform Responsa #34* and *#35*). In most instances in which this has been discussed the terminal patient is no longer capable of making rational decisions and must rely completely on those who are providing treatment. In this instance we are dealing with an individual who has made her wishes known.

We may understand the role which the patient and the physician play in their inter-relationship by looking at the frequently discussed theme of treatment for illness overriding various religious obligations. It has long been permitted to violate the Sabbath laws not only in order to save a life but even for someone who is dying (*Yoma* 84b; I. Lampronti *Pahad Yitzhaq, Holeh Beshabbat* etc). The general principle is that if either the physician or the patient believe that a treatment is required, and there is some risk to life, then the normal religious legislation is suspended *(Shulhan Arukh Orah Hayim* 328.5 and commentaries). The decision favored the patient who considered a treatment necessary even if a hundred doctors considered it not sufficiently urgent to override religious obligations, "because a heart knows its own bitterness." This and other discussions indicate that the patient is heavily involved in the treatments and not merely a quiet and subservient recipient.

In the instance of our patient, proper persuasion might have brought the widow to dialysis eight years ago. The fact that she lived eight years without dialysis at this advanced age may indicate that she chose the appropriate path for herself. Now as she is suffering from end stage renal disease, as well as congestive heart failure, it is not a question of saving her life, but possibly prolonging it at the expense of her dignity and with some pain both physical and psychological.

This patient rejected dialysis while living independently at home; and should not have dialysis imposed upon her now that she is dependent upon the services of a nursing home. Her attitude has led to a full, long life. Additional medical attention which she does not wish should not be forced on her; it is only likely to shorten her life. The physician has done his duty by suggesting the treatment. The patient knows that she is close to the end of her life - with or without the treatment - and is not obligated to accept the suggestion.

November 1988

*Walter Jacob, *Questions and Reform Jewish Answers - New American Reform Responsa*, New York, 1992, # 157.

SURGERY AT NINETY-SIX

Walter Jacob

QUESTION: A ninety-six-year-old woman who lives in a nursing home has recently been informed that severe hardening of the arteries necessitates the amputation of her foot. As a result of the shock of hearing this news, she has become severely disoriented. Her family was subsequently advised of her situation and several alternatives were presented. She may submit to amputation with a chance that her condition will be permanently corrected. However, there is no assurance that she may not die during surgery or soon thereafter. Furthermore, her other foot may be similarly affected, or her rehabilitation may not be successful. The alternative is a slow and painful death which can be partially relieved by sedation. The family wants the mother to make the decision. She refuses to sign the release for surgery. But as her lucid moments are brief, it is not clear whether that is what she actually wishes. Should there be surgery or should matters simply be allowed to take their course? (Rabbi, Illinois)*

ANSWER: We shall look at both the traditional and modern components of this question. Rabbinic tradition from Talmudic times onward has encouraged the utilization of all possible medical procedures for life threatening situations. *Sanhedrin* (23a) advocates this direction on the basis of "you shall not stand idly by the blood of your fellow" (Lev. 19.16). *Baba Kama* (85a) bases itself on "he shall cause him to be thoroughly healed" (Ex. 21.20). There are other parallel passages in which the citations are a little less clear. Nahmanides, (13th century) in his commentary on Leviticus 25.36 ("and your brother shall live with you"), followed this path, earlier proposed by Hai Gaon (10th century). Yehuda Lev Zirelson (20th century) applied this line of reasoning to less dangerous, non-life threatening situations (*Teshuvat Atzei Levanon #61*). The general principle that medical intervention is to be widely used has thus been established.

We must ask three further questions. Is this appropriate when the procedure is dangerous? Is there an age limit beyond which tradition would not advocate rigorous medical intervention? Shall this ninety-six-year-old woman face the trauma of an amputation?

The fact that considerable risk may be undertaken to save or restore life is based on a Talmudic discussion (*A. Z.* 27b), which interprets a story from II Kings (7.3 f). In this tale a group of lepers about to starve in the siege of Samaria decided to risk the mercy of the Syrian army rather than face certain death in the city. The Talmud used this discussion to show that in life threatening situations one might place oneself even into the hands of idolaters. In modern times this passage has been cited in order to permit the use of drugs whose side effects may be hazardous (J. Reischer, *Shevut Yaakov* III, #85; Posner, *Bet Meir Yoreh Deah* 339.1). There are further discussions about use of hazardous drugs when the chance of survival is low. Eliezer Waldenberg (*Tzitz Eliezer* 10, #25, Chap. 5, Sec. 5) felt that a 50% survival rate was necessary to recommend usage. Others like Mosheh Feinstein (*Igrot Mosheh, Yoreh Deah* 2, #59) felt that hazardous procedures and drugs may be used even when there is only a remote chance of survival. This path was also followed by I. Y. Unterman (*Noam* 12, p. 5). There is considerable debate on this matter. It is quite clear, however, that the use of medical procedures with a high risk have been encouraged by traditional Judaism whenever there is an opportunity to save a life.

In the literature cited, and in other instances, there has been no discussion of an age limit beyond which such procedures should not be utilized. If this individual is close to death, she should be permitted to die peacefully, and it is not necessary to subject her to needless pain through therapy which can not succeed (*Sefer Hasidim* #723; W. Jacob ed., *American Reformn Responsa, #* 79). However, if there is a chance for success, it should be undertaken.

Although the life span throughout the rabbinic and Biblical period was low, the Psalmist's ideal of three score years and ten, or by reason of strength four score years (Ps. 90) and Moses' life of one hundred and twenty with his "eyes undimmed and his vigor unabated" (Deut. 34. 7), as well as the ages of patriarchs and others, pointed to the ideal of an advanced age. As medical practice has advanced and made a longer life possible, we, too, should encourage medical procedures on individuals who have reached an advanced age.

However, we must also take into consideration the psychological factors which our forefathers only partially considered. In this instance even the news of a possible amputation was devastating, and the woman was not able to overcome it. This indicates a doubtful prognosis for her future. Here the psychological disadvantages may outweigh the medical advantages. We must remember that the efforts of tradition were solely concerned with saving life and not with its quality.

The medical prognosis is doubtful in our case and the psychological prognosis negative. Under these circumstances we would be reluctant to encourage an operation and inclined to let the woman live out her remaining days with the help of drug therapy to provide all possible comfort.

September 1984

*Walter Jacob, *Contemporary American Reform Responsa*, New York, 1987, # 85.

175

CPR AND THE FRAIL ELDERLY

Walter Jacob

QUESTION: When elderly patients in a nursing home or hospital are in need of cardio-pulmonary resuscitation is it advisable to initiate it among the frail elderly who are less likely to survive hospitalization subsequent to CPR than a younger person and who may even if they recover, be more frail and debilitated with a poorer quality of life? Should the patient or the official representative of the patient be able to indicate whether CPR should be initiated? What should the policy of long-term care institutions be in connection with Jewish patients? Should we make a distinction between patients who are likely to survive a year or more and those whose life span will be less? (Rabbi Lennard R. Thal, Los Angeles CA)*

ANSWER: Traditional Judaism has been very careful about judgments of life and death. In earlier times and at the present it remains difficult for the medical profession to predict the length of life. We have all seen cases in which the general prognosis is poor, but the spirit or physical condition of the patient enables that individual to survive considerable longer. Furthermore while some diseases rapidly take their toll among the elderly, others move much more slowly among them.

It is also virtually impossible to assess such matters as "the quality of life" and so Judaism has refrained from doing so. What might seem a very poor quality of life for some may be acceptable to others. In addition we must reckon with longer or shorter periods of depression which may strike such individuals either in the natural course of events or due to medication.

For these reasons and the general respect for life we have made no judgments on "quality of life" and would not consider that as a factor in instituting CPR or any other medical measures.

We should make a distinction between the frail elderly and a *goses* (a dying individual). Nothing needs to be done for someone who is clearly and obviously dying and whose death is close. At that stage we may not remove life support systems, but we also need not institute any procedures. There is a long tradition for allowing individuals not only a return to health but also a peaceful death.

Already in Talmudic times the pupil of Rabbi Judah Hanasi stopped his colleagues' prayers so he could die more comfortably (*Ketubot* 104a) and one may pray for death (Nisim Gerondi to *Nedarim* 40a). While in another instance a servant stopped the chopping of wood as the rhythmic beat of the axe disturbed the passage of the individual from this world (*Sefer Hassidim #723*).

The chief problem with a *goses* lies in the final stages when family, medical personnel, and hospitals may not know how to proceed and may fear legal or other consequences. This situation may be helped through some form of a "Living Will" which would describe the condition under which no further direct medical assistance should be provided. There are problems with the "Living Will" too. They have been described and discussed in another responsum in this volume. This is probably the best vehicle we now possess to deal with these issues.

The frail elderly should understand that they may amend or totally reject this document at any time. That is particularly important for individuals in a nursing home who may not have relatives nearby. In this way they will feel in control of their future rather than having the nursing home staff control their lives.

Under normal circumstance CPR should be given to the frail elderly if it can prolong their life. It should not be given to a *goses*.

April 1989

Walter Jacob, Questions and Reform Jewish Answers - New American Reform Responsa, New York, 1992, # 160.

PHYSICIAN KEEPING THE TRUTH FROM A PATIENT

Israel Bettan

QUESTION: As a physician I know that in being truthful with my patients I retain their confidence as well as my own self-respect. But it is not always possible for me to disclose all I know or have reason to suspect. I feel at times that the interest of my patient is better served if I withhold from him information of a shocking nature.

Having lived all my life in religious surroundings, I have often wondered what Jewish religion has to say on the subject. Am I ever justified, on religious grounds, in keeping the truth from my patients?*

ANSWER: Our ancient teachers, from whose utterances we draw deep draughts of wisdom even today, often voiced the conviction that religion was the handmaid rather than the lord of life. They held, for example, that with the exception of a number of vital negative commandments, the injunction to live in accord with the law precluded any situation in which complete obedience might prove perilous to life and health (*Sifra, Lev.* 18:5).

It is not strange, therefore, to hear these pious men express the view that in order to preserve peaceful relations among men, the bare truth may be given an appropriate disguise. In fact, they discover that on one occasion God Himself, to forestall any possible discord between Abraham and Sarah, deviated from the line of strict veracity (*Yevamot* 65b).

This general attitude finds embodiment in some legal enactments of the Rabbis. We are enjoined, for example, from apprising a sick person of the death of a close member of his family, lest the mental disturbance aggravate his condition (*Shulhan Arukh, Yoreh Deah* 337). Again, when one is about to die, and confession of his sins is in order, he shall be summoned to this last rite in a hopeful tone and in an atmosphere free from any display of grief. The prescribed formula reads: "Many men, after having made their final confession, continued to live;

many others, having failed to confess, also failed to recover. You who are about to confess your sins will surely be rewarded with renewed life. Also, confession assures one of his due portion of the world to come" (*ibid.*, 338).

The physician, who respects the truth and maintains truthful relations with all men, need have no qualms of conscience when, in certain special cases, in the pursuit of the good of a patient, he complies with the requirements of the situation and suppresses what appears to him to be the truth.

*Walter Jacob, *American Reform Responsa* ed., New York, 1983, # 74.

INFORMING A DYING PATIENT

Walter Jacob

QUESTION: The children have been informed that their mother is dying, and the physician believes that it is his responsibility to inform their mother of the hopelessness of her condition. The children have insisted that this news be kept from her as they feel it will hasten her death and make the last period of her life miserable. Which path should be followed? (Norman Levin, Cleveland OH)*

ANSWER: It is our principle task during illness, including the final illness, to maintain an attitude of hope in the patient. Therefore, the rabbinic tradition rejected the approach of the prophet Isaiah to King Hezekiah in which he demanded that the king "set his house in order, for you will die and not live" (II Kings 20.1). Actually the king was healed and survived. The Talmudic discussion of such situations felt that prayer and hope should not cease even when the outlook was bleak (*Ber.* 10a). In another Biblical story which the rabbis quoted, the prophet Elijah was asked whether Ben Hadad the Aramean King would recover, and he lied to encourage him (II Kings 8.10 f). We may therefore stretch the truth to engender hope. This mood of hopefulness was carried even further by the injunction not to inform a seriously ill patient of the death of a relative as that might change her mood *(Shulhan Arukh Yoreh Deah* 377).

We must, of course, weigh this attitude against that of giving the patient sufficient time to prepare her affairs before death and also the opportunity to make confession (*Semahot* 4.1; *M. Sanhedrin* 6.2; 32a). In this instance there are no pressing business affairs which need to be settled. Personal confession can occur at any time; it need not be formalized into an occasion which will frighten the mother. The physician has done his duty by speaking of the condition to the children. If the mother inquires repeatedly from the physician and indicates that she wishes to know the truth, then she should be told to her. If that does not occur we should follow the path of Tradition and the inclination of the children and allow the mother to retain her currently hopeful attitude.

July 1988

*Walter Jacob, *Questions and Reform Jewish Answers, New American Reform Responsa*, New York, 1992, # 158

DETERMINATION AND POSTPONEMENT OF DEATH

Solomon B. Freehof

QUESTION: What are the religious connotations of the fact that an artificial heart may for a time revive a patient whose heart has stopped beating? Or if a patient is revived after irreparable damage has been done to the brain, would such action be deemed justified by Jewish religious tradition? (Question referred by Nelson Glueck, Cincinnati, OH)*

ANSWER: The various matters involved here have all become actual and practical due to modern methods of resuscitating those apparently dead. They involve many ethical and traditional problems as the questions quite properly indicate.

First of all, what does tradition consider physical evidence of death? When has death actually occurred? This question became a practical one almost two hundred years ago when laws were passed in various Central European countries prohibiting the traditional Jewish custom of burying the dead on the very day of death. These new laws had in mind the possibility that a patient may seem to be dead and not really be dead and that, therefore, there must be no burial before three days have passed. When Moses Mendelssohn was asked, he argued that a three day delay was permissible by Jewish law. Jacob Emden proved the opposite, namely, that it was not permissible to delay burial. Later when the same decree was passed in the Austro-Hungarian Empire, other incidental problems were involved. For example, could a doctor who was a *Kohen* examine the dead to see that they are actually dead? Could he examine the body two days after the apparent death, which the law would require and which Jewish law forbids to a *Kohen*?

This question was taken up by the great Hungarian authority, Moses Sofer, in his *Responsa, Yoreh Deah, #338*, and his chief proof is based upon tradition, namely, that our people who deal with the burial (the *Hevrah Qadisha*) have an inherited tradition of ancient wisdom and they can tell whether the person is really dead or not. That test is mainly whether there is any breathing. When the breathing has finished and the pulse has ceased, the person is declared dead. This assumption of an ancient, inherited wisdom was a natural one for Moses Sofer to make in defense of the Jewish custom of burial on the day of death. (For a full discussion of this responsum, see *Treasury of Responsa,* p. 236 ff.)

All this, of course, deals merely with fixing the moment of death. But the law is concerned, also, with an earlier situation, namely, the state of such people who are so badly injured or so sick as to be definitely in a dying condition with no probability of long survival. In other words, there is a great deal of debate as to when a person, although living, no longer has real viability. Such a person is called *terefah* by analogy with an animal which is torn by beasts and thus called *terefah.* Which injuries in an animal make it virtually a dying animal and therefore prohibited for food? The main injuries and ailments are considered traditional from Moses from Mount Sinai (*Hulin* 43a top). Maimonides elaborates the list of traditional evidences of moribundity to an enumeration of seventy such ailments *(Hil. Shehitah* X, 9). Do such injuries apply to human beings also? In other words, if a person has such an injury or ailment is he considered to be already in dying condition? There is disagreement in the law among the scholars as to whether that is so. A convenient summary of the differing opinions of the Tosafists on this question is to be found in the commentary of Yom Tov Lipmann Heller, to *Yevamot* XVI, 4. In general, they may disagree about certain animal ailments or injuries, whether they are a mark of moribundity when found in man, but by and large they accept the standards set down for animals, namely, that if a person (as is in the case with animals) cannot be expected to live more than twelve months, such a person is considered to be in a dying condition.

These discussions of whether a person is to be considered *terefah,* i.e., moribund, have bearing on practical legal questions. Chaim Alfandari, in his *Responsa, Magid Mereshit, #2,* presents an interesting question involved here. A man may not marry his wife's sister if his wife is still alive, but after she dies there is no such prohibition. The question asked here was the following: A man's wife was moribund and he gave *qidushin* to his wife's sister. Are these *qidushin* valid on the ground that his first wife, being moribund, is to be considered as legally dead? (The conclusion, incidentally, is that such *qidushin* are prohibited.)

A fuller discussion of the question of moribundity in man is given again by Moses Sofer in his *Responsa, Yoreh Deah #52*. It begins with a question of an animal that was shot with bird-shot and lived longer that the period of twelve months. Is the animal to be considered *terefah* and therefore unfit for food? After discussing this primary question, he goes into the question of the extent to which these rules of *terefah* animals apply to man, and he says, of course, that man may survive certain ailments and injuries which would be fatal in animals, because of the belief that man has a protecting angel or good luck, *adam it lei mazala. (Shabat* 53a) And sometimes medicines applied to a human being will cure him. On the other hand, he says, in some ways man is weaker than animals and the various injuries, etc., mentioned as fatal apply all the more to man than they do to animals.

The questions asked involve also the matter of brain injuries. It is interesting to note that this question is also asked and discussed in the Talmud. For example, a brain injury would declare an animal *terefah* but with a man it would have to be not only a fracture of the skull but also an injury to the lining of the brain (cf. Tos. to *Hulin* 42b) . And also, the Talmud in *Hulin* 57b tells of an incident that happened in the town of En Bol, where a man had a hole in his head and they made him a plug of gourd shell and he lived. But one rabbi says that the patient lived only because that event occurred in the summer but when the winter came he died.

Out of all this discussion they have a general standard of moribundity. First the one in the Mishnah, *Hulin* III, 1, that when similar injuries are fatal in others, these injuries, wherever they occur, are deemed fatal. And, secondly, the rule that those that are not likely to survive twelve months are considered to be moribund *(terefah)*. Now the practical ethical problem is this: Whatever their ancient rules were as to moribundity, we must understand that the rules of analogy with animals were not deemed absolute and as Moses Sofer says, by good fortune and by medicine certain ailments can be cured.

Our question becomes more specific: Is there a point where it would be considered morally wrong to apply modern devices? Let us say a patient is dying of cancer and is in great pain, and his heart has blessedly stopped; is it morally right to revive him, as can often be done, only that he may suffer longer? There is a general principle on this question which is derivable from Jewish tradition. It goes back to the narrative in the Talmud, *Ketuvot* 104a. Rabbi Judah the Prince was dying in great suffering. The rabbis insisted on ceaselessly praying so that he be kept alive a little longer; but his famous servant-woman (who is often referred to with honor in the Talmud) threw an earthen jar from the roof in the midst of the praying rabbis in order to stop their prayers so that Rabbi Judah might peacefully die. The Spanish scholar, Nissim Gerondi (to *Nedarim* 40a top), says that while it is our duty to pray for a sick person that he may recover, there come times when we should pray for God's mercy that he may die. So, too, in *Sefer Hasidim,* #315-318, basing its opinion on the statement of Ecclesiastes: "There is a time to live and a time to die," says as follows: "If a man is dying, do not pray too hard that his soul return and that he revive from the coma. He can at best live only a few days and in those days he will endure great suffering. So, 'there is a time to die.' " (See other such references in *Reform Responsa,* p. 117 ff.) In other words, according to the spirit of Jewish tradition just as a man has the right to live, so there come times when he has a right to die. And we have no right to deprive him of that peaceful departure. The *Shulhan Arukh, Yoreh Deah* 339, makes it clear that while we may do nothing to *hasten* death, we should not do anything to prevent its coming when it is inevitable.

The basic question here involved is: How much importance should we give to the last few hours of life of a dying man? Would we consider these last few hours so important that we would encourage the doctor to give him stimulants to keep him alive for another half hour and another half hour?

The chief source of the discussion is derivable from the Talmud in *Avodah Zarah* 27b, where the question is whether a Jew should submit to the medical attention of a heathen healer. The question arose because the heathens in those days would be suspected of putting the Jewish patient to death. So, too, a heathen was not permitted to circumcise. Of course this does not apply to Christian doctors, nor even in the case of heathens to a physician of proven skill. It applies to a heathen healer whose skill is dubious and whose motives are questionable. In discussing the question whether to use even such a dangerous pagan healer, the answer is that it depends on how sick the Jew is. If there is a fair chance that he might recover, that is, if the probabilities are equally balanced whether he will live or whether he will die, then we may not risk that fifty-fifty chance and employ the dangerous pagan. But if it is strongly probable that he is dying anyhow, then the risk of using the help of the pagan is permitted. The reason given in the Talmud for this distinction is stated as a principle, namely, "We do not put too much importance on the last moments of life," *En mashgihin lehayei shaah.* In other words, the last few moments of a dying man might as well be risked since they are not of too much importance. So, too, the law is stated in Maimonides, *Yad Hil. Rotzeah,* XII, 9, and so in the *Shulhan Arukh, Yoreh Deah* 155, #1.

Of course the principle that "we do not put too much importance on the last moments of life," *hayei shaah,* does not mean that we may *hasten* death. That is clearly forbidden. We may not hasten death by any action. To that extent, we *do* care for the last hour; but on the other hand, if there is a fair chance that a person may actually be healed from his sickness, we may risk that last hour. This willingness to take a chance with the last hour for the sake of healing is clearly stated by Nachmanides in his *Torat Haadam,* p. 11d (Venice ed.) He says we disregard the dubiousness of "the life of the hour" (i.e., the last dying hour) in the face of the possibility that he might live for a considerable time.

This willingness to risk the last hours of life, which the Talmud in *Avodah Zarah* mentions as a regular rule, was applied practically in at least two instances in the responsa literature. Jacob Reischer of Metz d. 1733) in his *Shevut Yaakov*, III, #75, had exactly such a question. The person was, in the doctor's judgment, now dying. He had only one or two days to live. There was, however, a new medicine that could perhaps cure him, enabling him to live for a long time, but it might also kill him. Reischer, according to the principles mentioned above, said that while we may not in general hasten death, if however the doctors agree that there is a fair chance that he may be cured for a good extension of his life, then we should risk this last day of his life. Precisely the same question has come up recently in a responsum by Jacob Breisch of Zurich, Switzerland, in his newly appeared volume III, responsum #141. He comes to the same conclusion as did Jacob Reischer two centuries before.

The principle, therefore, is clear enough. These last few hours of life, *hayei shaah,* are not so important in the ethics of the *halakhah* that we may keep on preventing a person from dying, just in order to gain another hour or two. Of course, for a fair probability of *cure,* we must try all means and methods and even risk for a probable cure wiping out of his last hour or two.

Greater knowledge of the human body enables us to define much more closely than the rabbis of the past did when a person is actually moribund or whether he still has viability. We also have new remedies such as heart-pacers, adrenalin, etc. Nevertheless, the ethical principle underlying the Jewish tradition seems strong, although, of course, applied somewhat differently today. The ethics of the law would be substantially as follows: If the modern methods of revival bring with them a fair probability that the patient may recover some health for, let us say, twelve months (as their old test had it) and be fairly free of pain and be able to live a life of some activity, then the remedy is justified and the patient should be revived. But if these methods merely revive a patient for a longer period of pain, or continued weeks or even months of moribundity, then they are contrary to the spirit of Jewish ethical-legal tradition.

*Solomon B. Freehof, *Modern Reform Responsa*, Cincinnati, 1971, # 34.

PASSIVE EUTHANASIA

Moshe Zemer

QUESTION: A man, age forty, was suffering from amyotrophic lateral sclerosis which is characterized by progressive paralysis of his muscles. At the terminal stage the patient cannot swallow of use his muscles any more. He is in extreme pain and discomfort. The prognosis is certain and irreversible. The patient appealed to the District Court of Tel Aviv for an injunction against his physician and hospital to refrain from connecting him to a lung-heart machine. The injunction was granted. W member of the Israel Movement for Progressive Judaism asked whether such a decision would be contrary to the position of the *halakhah*.

ANSWER: In Jewish tradition there is a severe conflict between two spiritual values:

One value is the sanctity of life, *qedushat hahayim*, of every human being. To save this life one may transgress all the commandments of the Torah except three: murder, incest and idolatry.

The other is the concern and compassion for the suffering of a person created in the image of God. Many *mitzvot* have been put aside in order to alleviate this suffering and to preserve human dignity - *kevod habriyot*.

There are times that when you preserve a person's life, you prolong his unbearable suffering. On the other hand, there are situations in which the only relief from this suffering is in death. finding relief may be in ending

Euthanasia involves a series of complex and varied phenomena and activities. I shall confine my responsum to the form that fits our question namely passive euthanasia. I shall, however, briefly mention two other forms that will shed light on our case.

There is well the known case of Rabbi Yehudah HaNasi's maidservant who prayed for his recovery. However, when she realized how great was his suffering she prayed that he be released from his agony and even disturbed Rabbi's disciples in their prayers so they ceased praying for a moment and the soul of Rabbi's soul departed to its eternal rest (*Ketubot* 104a).

R. Nissim b. Reuben Gerondi (Spain, d. 1380) commented on this: "There are times when one should ask for mercy for the ill that he may die; such as in the case where he is suffering greatly and there is no hope that he may recover and live just as in the case of rabbi and his maidservant" (Nedarim 40a).

We may see that this prayerful euthanasia was taken seriously by those who believed in the efficacy of prayer. Another example is the Midrash about a very old lady who wished to depart from this world. R. Yossi recommended that she refrain from going to the synagogue for three consecutive days, and as a result she became ill and died (*Yalkut Shemoni*, Proverbs, 943).

The Talmud and rabbinic codes state that a *goses*, a dying patient whose demise is imminent, is regarded as a living person in all respects. Nothing may be done to hasten his death. It is forbidden to wash the patient, remove the pillow from underneath him, to place him on the ground. It is also forbidden to close his eyes "for whoever closes the eyes with the onset of death is a shedder of blood." Furthermore, the keys of the synagogue may not be put under his head so that he may depart (*Shulhan Arukh, Yoreh Deah*, 339:1).

Each of these acts is forbidden because the slightest movement of the patient may hasten death. As the Babylonian Talmud put it: "This action may be compared to a flickering flame; as soon as one touches it, the light is extinguished." This is called *hariga bayadayim*, literally "killing with one's hands or in modern parlance, active euthanasia.

These prohibitions apply even in the case where the dying person might be deprived of only a few minutes of life: *hayei shaah*. The Talmud teaches us: If a wall falls on a person on Shabbat, the victim trapped under the debris is to be rescued even if as a result of such efforts his life will be prolonged only by a matter of moments (*Yoma* 85a). Not only is every human life is immeasurable precious.

Passive euthaniasia appears in two forms:

A. *Shev ve-al taaseh* - Take no action, remain passive, in contrast to the active approach, *qum ve'aseh*, of active euthanasia. This usually refers to the situation before the patient is connected to the heart-lung machine or given intravenous feeding.

Solomon B. Freehof wrote a responsum in 1969 about a terminal patient who was dying as a result of a series of strokes. Two physicians, one of whom was the patient's son, decided - with the consent of the family - to hasten the end by withdrawing all medication and fluids given intravenokusly. Rabbi Freehof conswented, but suggested that it would be preferable if the hiosp[ital's practice tohave each day's intravenous feeding kept up by the direct daily order of the physicain, and if,on a particular day, it was decided that it should cease, the doctor simply refrains from ordering it to be continued. Thus, in no way would he be traking any direction. Here, then, the Talmudic principle *Shev ve-al taaseh adif* (it is preferable to desist from direct action) would certainly apply (W. Jacob, (ed.) *American Reform Responsa #77*).

B. The second form of passive euthanasia is the removal of the impediment (*Le-hasir et hamonea*). R. Moses Isserles of Crakow, 16th century, decided that if these is anything which causes a hindrance to the departure of the soul, such as the knocking noise of wood chopping, or salt on the patient's tongue, and these hinder the soul's departure, it is permissible to remove them. here is no act involved in this at all, but only the removal of the impediment (*Shulhan Arukh*).

R. Zvi Hirsch b. Azriel of Vilna explains this removal of the obstacle: It is forbidden to delay his death and they should not have put salt on his tongue to keep him from dying...therefore, it is permitted to remove the salt from his tongue (*Beit Lehem Yehudah*,to *Shulhan Arukh*, 1804).

R. Yaakov b. Shmuel of Seusmer (Dyhernfuerth), Prussia, wrote in his *Responsa, Beit Yaakov* (1696): "It is forbidden to delay the soul's departure and the demise of the dying person. One must not use medication in order to prolong the dying process."

In contrast to this decision, R. Yaakov b. Yose Reisher stated that an expert in medication that would delay the dying process even for a few moments is permitted to give such medicine to the patient. It is similar to our clearing away the debris on Shabbat to add a few minutes to the life of the victim (*Responsa, Shevut Yaakov* III:13).

We find support for the second form of passive euthanasia among modern Israeli decisors. R. Baruch Rabinowitz, Chief Rabbi of Holon stated that this *halakhah* (of removing the impediment to death) is very important in the process of modern healing:

In most cases, when efforts are made to save the patient, he is connected to various sorts of instruments to enable him to breathe and given many forms of medication. As long as; his body is connected to these instruments, he can continue for a long period to live, what physicians call "vegetative life." However, who are not able to distinguish between vegetative life on the one hand and rational-emotional life on the other. The question therefore arises, are we permitted to disconnect the instruments from the patient as long as he shows signs of life. The physician, in truth, has already despaired of restoring the patient to natural and spontaneous life, but this artificially sustained life can continue. Is it permitted for the doctor to disconnect and make them cease ? That is he problem with which we are confronted in the hospital every day. Many doctors ask what they should do, because the moment that they disconnect - the patient dies. Is this not a form of active killing?

The above mentioned *halakhah* distinguishes between shortening the life of a *goses* and removing the impediment which delays the departure of the soul (death): that is the artificial prolongation of the life of a dying person and thereby gives us a clear answer to the question. The instrument artificially delays death. After the physician has reached the conclusion, that there is no more possibility of natural life in the person and that he is indeed moribund, a *goses*, the action of the instrument is only preventing the departure of his soul, it is only artificially prolonging the sate of dying. Therefore, the person must be disconnected from the respirator or other instrument and leave him in a natural state until he dies." (*Assia* Vol. 1, 1979, pp. 197f.)

R. Haim David Halevi, Sephardic Chief Rabbi of Tel Aviv, wrote: "Not only is it permitted to disconnect him from artificial respiration, but it is compulsory to do so because the person's soul which belongs to God has already been taken by his Maker, for immediately when the respirator is removed, he will die." (Responsa *Aseh Lecha Rav* V:29)

We may, therefore, see that medieval and modern respondents made *halakhic* decisions in consonance with the verdict of the Tel Aviv District Court.

There would be no better way to conclude this responsum than with the words of Justice Haim Cohn, a member of the Academic Council of our Institute, taken from the coda of his essay "On the Dichotomy of Divinity and Humanity in Jewish Law" in *Euthanasia* (ed. Amnon Carmi).

The golden rule of Biblical law, "Thou shalt love thy neighbour as thyself" was interpreted by the Talmudic jurists as imposing a duty to choose for one's fellowman the most "Beautiful" death possible *mitah yafah*, (*San.* 45a, 52a-b). In practice, the application of the rule was originally confined to choices among several possible modes of execution.... Both the reasoning behind the talmudic rule and its comprehensive language allow it to be applied more generally to every situation in which man (usually the physician) is faced with a choice between two kinds of death to be caused to his fellowman - the one agonizing and protracted, the other relatively east, swift, and humane. This most fundamental of all divine commands (*B.R.* 24:7 in the name of R. Akiba) exhorts one to conduct oneself, especially in the face of death, in such a manner as may be dictated by sincere love for the dying person....

The Midrash relates that in the law book (*Torah*) of R. Meir was written the following version of the conclusion of the creation story of Genesis:N "And God saw everything that he had made and behold it was good." What was it that God, seeing all of His creation, that he beheld to be very good? It was death. R. Meir's version read *vehinei tov mot*, and behold good is the death. (B. R. 9:5)....

Justice Cohn concluded: "Might it be that surveying the whole of His magnificent creation, a merciful God consoled himself with how good and comforting it was that having created man, He had created death to rescue man from life?"

November 1990   Moshe Zemer, *Halakhah Shefuyah*, Tel Aviv, 1993, pp. 295-298.

ALLOWING A TERMINAL PATIENT TO DIE

Solomon B. Freehof

QUESTION: A terminal patient was dying as a result of a series of strokes. Two physicians, one of whom was the patient's son, decided - with the consent of the family - to hasten the end by withdrawing all medication and fluids given intravenously. Is such procedure permitted by Jewish law?*

ANSWER: This is a complex question and, therefore, is not quite clear in the law. However, there is enough in the legal literature to permit us to arrive at a conclusion.

First, let us dispose of a secondary question. It is not altogether irrelevant that one of the physicians, a noted surgeon, was the son of the patient. There is a great deal of discussion in Jewish law as to the relationship between a physician and a patient who is his father. There are many responsa which--even nowadays-discuss the question whether a son who is a surgeon may operate on his father.

The basis of this legal debate is Exodus 21:15, which states that he who smites his father must be pu. to death; and the law is that "smiting" is not considered so grave a sin unless it creates a wound. Therefore it is the creating of a wound on the body of one's father which is considered a grave sin. Hence the Mishnah (*Sanhedrin* XI.I) and the Talmud (*Sanhedrin* 84b) discuss whether a son may perform the operation of bloodletting on his father as part of his work as a physician, or make a wound on his body. This is discussed by Maimonides in *Yad, Hilhkot Mamrim*, V.7, and in the *Shulhan Arukh, Yoreh Deah* 241.3. In the *Shulhan Arukh*, Caro states the law that a son may not operate on a father, but Isserles says that if there is no one else available for the operation, he may do so. Isserles bases his opinion on the opinion of Maimonides (*loc. cit.*). This would be the general conclusion of the law. All this, of course, is incidental to our question.

The real question is: What is the limit on the freedom of action of a physician with regard to a dying patient? By "dying patient" we do not mean a patient who is in danger of death but only one who can yet be healed. If, for example, a person has a heart attack and can be healed (as many are from one attack or even two), or if a patient has been rescued from drowning and can be saved with resuscitation (but if no resuscitation is given he will die) - such dying patients, all of whom have a prospect for recovery, must be given the full resources of medicine in the attempt to save them. One may even risk a remedy that might possibly kill them, provided there is a fair chance that the remedy might save them. Thus, the Talmud (*Avodah Zarah* 27b) says clearly that one may risk otherwise forbidden remedies (e.g., from a heathen healer) if the dying patient has a chance to be cured by the remedy. See the full discussion of this permission to risk death if there is a fair chance to cure in *Shevut Yaakov* III.75 (Jacob Reischer of Metz, d. 1733).

But in the case under consideration we are not dealing with a dying patient who has a chance for recovery if given the proper medication. We are dealing with a patient with regard to whom all the physicians present, including his own son, agree that he has no chance for recovery. In other words, he is a *terminal* patient. What, then, are the limits of freedom of action of a physician with a terminal patient?

Is it the physician's duty to keep this hopeless patient (who is also in all likelihood suffering great pain) alive a little longer, maybe a day or two? Jewish law is quite clear on this question. He is not in duty bound to force him to live a few more days or hours. This law is based on the famous incident in *Ketubot* 104a. Rabbi Judah the Prince was dying in great suffering. The Rabbis insisted on ceaselessly praying so that he might thus be kept alive a little longer. But his servant-woman (who is often referred to with honor in the Talmud) threw down an earthen jar from the roof of the house into the midst of the praying Rabbis, in order to stop their prayers so that Rabbi Judah might peacefully die. The Spanish scholar Nissim Gerondi (to *Nedarim* 40a, top)says that while it is our duty to pray for a sick person that he may recover, there comes a time when we should pray for God's mercy that he should die. So, too, *Sefer Hasidim* (#315-318, edition Frankfurt),

198

basing its opinion on the statement of Ecclesiastes, "There is a time to live and a time to die", says as follows: "If a man is dying, we do not pray too hard that his soul return and that he revive from the coma; he can at best live only a few days and in those days will endure great suffering; so 'there is a time to die.'" (See other such references in *Reform Responsa*, pp. 117ff). In other words, according to the spirit of Jewish tradition, just as a man has a right to live, so there comes a time when he has a right to die. Thus, there is no duty incumbent upon the physician to force a terminal patient to live a little longer.

But what, under these circumstances, is a physician permitted actually to do? Here again the law is clear. He may do nothing positive to hasten death. The Mishnah (*Shabbat* XXIII.5) says that we may not close the eyes of a dying patient. The Talmud (*Shabbat* 151b) compares the dying patient to a guttering candle that is about to go out. If a man touches his fingertip to the candle flame, it will go out at once. This he must not do. In other words, he must not hasten the death of a dying patient by closing his eyes. The Talmudic discussion is elaborated on in the post-Talmudic treatise, *Semahot*, chapter 1, and finally is codified in the *Shulhan Arukh, Yoreh Deah* 339, where it is clear that no action must be taken to hasten death, i.e., you may not remove a pillow from under his head. However (see Isserles, *ibid.*), if someone outside is chopping wood and that rhythmic sound focuses the mind of the dying patient and prevents his soul from departing, you may stop the wood-chopping so that the patient may relax and die in peace. Or, if there is salt on the patient's tongue and the tartness of the salt focuses his mind and keeps him from relaxing into death, you may wipe the salt from his tongue and thus allow him to die. The Taz expresses some doubt about the permission to wipe the patient's tongue, for that would shake and disturb the patient and would be an overt act.

The fullest discussion as to what is a permitted act and what is a non-permitted act is found in *Shiltei Hagiborim* (Joshua Boaz) to *Moed Qatan*, third chapter (in Wilna edition, Alfasi, 16b). He concludes that while you must not do anything to hasten death, you may remove the causes of the delay of death. He bases his discussion upon the *Sefer Hasidim* (edition Frankfurt, #315), which says: "We may not put salt on his tongue in order to prevent his dying." And so Isserles in the *Shulhan Arukh (loc. cit.)* sums up what is permitted and what is not permitted by saying that such things are permitted "which do not involve action at all, but merely remove that which hinders the death."

All this brings us to a clearer understanding as to the limits of freedom of action of the physician in relation to the hopelessly dying patient. He may not take any overt action to hasten death, such as giving him, perhaps, an overdose of an opiate, but he may refrain from doing that which will prevent his dying. Of course, in this case, if he ordered the removal of the intravenous apparatus, there may be some ground for objection if the removal of the apparatus was a rather forcible procedure and shook up the patient. But if for example, the removal of the apparatus was so gentle as not to disturb him, it would be like the wiping off of the salt on his tongue, which Isserles permits. If he does not even do this, but merely gives the order that the bottle containing the nutriment not be refilled when it is emptied out, then, too, he committed no sin at all. He is merely, as the law says, preventing that which delays the death.

We have mentioned that Isserles states (*Yoreh Deah* 339.1) that one may remove that which prevents the person from dying, and thus, one may stop someone who is chopping wood outside because the regular sound concentrates the patient's mind, and one may also remove some salt from his lips. The Taz objects only to wiping away the salt from the lips, because this action might move or shake the patient, and this would be an overt action hastening his death.

On the basis of this objection of the Taz, there might be some question, as we have mentioned, about removing the tubes from his arm through which the intravenous feeding enters his body. Of course, if this is done gently, the objection of the Taz would be obviated. Perhaps it would be better still if the tubes were not removed at all until the patient were dead. There might also be some question if the intravenous feeding would be continued automatically until the physician gives a direct order that it be stopped. It would he less objectionable if it is the practice in the hospital to have each day's intravenous feeding kept up by the direct daily order of the physician, and if, on that particular day, he simply refrains from ordering it to be continued. Thus, in no way would he be taking any direct action. Here, then, the principle (*Eruvin* 100a) *shev ve-al taaseh adif* would certainly apply.

To sum up: If the patient is a hopelessly dying patient, the physician has no duty to keep him alive a little longer. He is entitled to die. If the physician attempts actively to hasten the death, that is against the ethics of Jewish law. In the case as described, the term used in the question, "to hasten death," is perhaps not correct, or at least should be modified. The physician is not really hastening the death; he has simply ceased his efforts to delay it.

*Walter Jacob, *American Reform Responsa* ed., New York, 1983, #77.

CONTRIBUTORS

Israel Bettan - (1889-1957), Professor of Midrash and Homiletics at the Hebrew Union College, Cincinnati, President of the Central Conference of American Rabbis, Chair of its Responsa Commitee. Author of *Studies in Jewish Preaching in the Middle Ages* (1939), *The Five Scrolls* (1950).

William Cutter - Professor of Education and Hebrew Literature at the Hebrew Union College-Jewish Institute of Religion in Los Angeles. He writes in hermeneutics and literary theory. He is Instructor in Chaplaincy and has developed professional education and pastoral programs.

Solomon B. Freehof - (1893-1990), Rabbi of the Rodef Shalom Congregation, President of the Central Conference of American Rabbis and the World Union for Progressive Judaism, Chair of the Responsa Committee of the Central Conference of American Rabbis. Author of eight volumes of responsa including *Today's Reform Responsa* (1990), as well as *Reform Jewish Practice* (1947, 1952), *The Responsa Literature* (1955), *A Treasury of Responsa* (1963).

Walter Jacob - Rabbi of the Rodef Shalom Congregation, Pittsburgh, Immediate past President of the Central Conference of American Rabbis, Chair of its Responsa Committee. President of the Freehof Institute of Progressive *Halakhah*. Author and editor of sixteen books including *American Reform Responsa* (1983), *Contemporary American Reform Responsa* (1987), *Liberal Judaism and Halakhah* (1988), *Questions and Reform Jewish Answers - New Reform Responsa* (1991).

Peter Knobel - Rabbi, Beth Emet, Evanston, Ill. Chair of the Liturgy Committee of the Central Conference of American Rabbis; Book-review Editor, *Journal of the Central Conference of American Rabbis.* Editor of *Gates of the Season* (1983).

Leonard Kravitz - Professor of Midrash and Homiletics at the Hebrew Union College - Jewish Institute of Religion in New York. He has served on the Medical Ethics Committee of the New York Federation of Jewish Philanthropies. Author of *The Esoteric Meaning of Maimonides' Guide for the Perplexed* (1988), *Commentary on the Ethics of the Father* (1992) with K. Olitzky.

Jacob Z. Lauterbach - (1873-1942), Professor of Talmud and Rabbinics, Hebrew Union College, Cincinnati. Chair of the Responsa Committee of the Central Conference of American Rabbis. Editor of *Mekhilta deRav Ishmael* (1933-49). Contributor to the *Jewish Encyclopedia*.

Mark N. Staitman - Associate Rabbi of the Rodef Shalom Congregation, Pittsburgh, PA. On the faculty of the Pittsburgh Theological Seminary; serves on the Bio-Medical Institutional Review Board of the University of Pittsburgh Medical Center and is a Visiting Fellow in its Center for Medical Ethics.

Moshe Zemer - Director of the Freehof Institute of Progressive *Halakhah*; a founder of the Movement for Progressive Judaism in Israel; *Av Bet Din* of the Israel Council of Progressive Rabbis. Founding Rabbi of Kedem Synagogue-Beit Daniel in Tel Aviv. Author of *The Sane Halakhah* (1993).

www.ingramcontent.com/pod-product-compliance
Lightning Source LLC
Chambersburg PA
CBHW060037030426
42334CB00019B/2376